Word in Our Time

About the authors

MARTIN KITCHEN is a graduate in modern languages and theology of the University of London and holds a doctorate in New Testament Studies from the University of Manchester. He prepared for ordination at King's College, London, and with the Southwark Ordination Course and is a Residentiary Canon of Durham Cathedral.

GEORGIANA HESKINS teaches Religious Studies at Eltham College, an independent school for boys in south east London. She is a priest-vicar at Southwark Cathedral and lives in the Borough of Greenwich, within sight of the Thames Barrier and the Millennium Dome. She was, until recently, Tutor at the South East Institute for Theological Education where she taught Pastoral and Biblical Studies. Her own preparation for ordination was at King's College, London, and at Westcott House in Cambridge, and most of her preaching experience has been gained in London.

STEPHEN MOTYER spent some years at the pulpit-face trying to make the lectionary live in rural Hertfordshire, before taking up his present post as New Testament Lecturer at London Bible College. Before that he taught at Oak Hill College, and looks back with thankfulness on theological studies at Cambridge, Bristol, Tübingen and London. With the other authors of this Commentary, he shares a vision for inspiring preaching at the heart of worship.

Word in Our Time

*Insights into the Scripture readings
for Sundays and Holy Days*

Year C

Martin Kitchen, Georgiana Heskins
and Stephen Motyer

CANTERBURY
PRESS
Norwich

© Martin Kitchen, Georgiana Heskins and Stephen Motyer,
2000
First published 2000 by The Canterbury Press Norwich
(a publishing imprint of Hymns Ancient & Modern Limited,
a registered charity)
St Mary's Works, St Mary's Plain,
Norwich, Norfolk, NR3 3BH

British Library Cataloguing in Publication Data

A catalogue record for this book is available
from the British Library

ISBN 1-85311-366-2

Typeset by Rowland Phototypesetting Limited,
Bury St Edmunds, Suffolk
Printed in Great Britain by
Biddles Limited, Guildford and King's Lynn

Contents

Preface   ix
Introduction: On Reading St Luke's Gospel   xi
List of Abbreviations of Bible Translations Cited   xiv

Word in Our Time

The First Sunday of Advent   1
The Second Sunday of Advent   3
The Third Sunday of Advent   5
The Fourth Sunday of Advent   8
Christmas Eve   11
Christmas Day: 13
   First set of readings   13
   Second set of readings   16
   Third set of readings   18
The First Sunday of Christmas   20
The Second Sunday of Christmas   22
The Epiphany   25
The Baptism of Christ: *The First Sunday of Epiphany*   28
The Second Sunday of Epiphany   30
The Third Sunday of Epiphany   32
The Fourth Sunday of Epiphany   35
The Presentation of Christ   37
Ordinary Time   39
  – Proper 1: *Sunday between 3 and 9 February*   39
  – Proper 2: *Sunday between 10 and 16 February*   41
  – Proper 3: *Sunday between 17 and 23 February*   44

The Second Sunday before Lent   47
The Sunday Next before Lent   49
Ash Wednesday   52
The First Sunday of Lent   54
The Second Sunday of Lent   57
The Third Sunday of Lent   59
The Fourth Sunday of Lent   62
Mothering Sunday   64
The Fifth Sunday of Lent   66
Palm Sunday   68
The Monday of Holy Week   70
The Tuesday of Holy Week   72
The Wednesday of Holy Week   74
Maundy Thursday   76
Good Friday   78
Easter Eve   80
Easter Day   82
The Second Sunday of Easter   84
The Third Sunday of Easter   86
The Fourth Sunday of Easter   89
The Fifth Sunday of Easter   91
The Sixth Sunday of Easter   93
Ascension Day   95
The Seventh Sunday of Easter   97
Day of Pentecost   99
Trinity Sunday   101
Day of Thanksgiving for Holy Communion: 103
   Thursday after Trinity Sunday (Corpus Christi)   103
Ordinary Time   105
   – Proper 4: *Sunday between 29 May and 4 June*   105
   – Proper 5: *Sunday between 5 and 11 June*   108
   – Proper 6: *Sunday between 12 and 18 June*   111
   – Proper 7: *Sunday between 19 and 25 June*   113
   – Proper 8: *Sunday between 26 June and 2 July*   116
   – Proper 9: *Sunday between 3 and 9 July*   119
   – Proper 10: *Sunday between 10 and 16 July*   121
   – Proper 11: *Sunday between 17 and 23 July*   123

– Proper 12: *Sunday between 24 and 30 July*   125
– Proper 13: *Sunday between 31 July and 6 August*   127
– Proper 14: *Sunday between 7 and 13 August*   129
– Proper 15: *Sunday between 14 and 20 August*   131
– Proper 16: *Sunday between 21 and 27 August*   133
– Proper 17: *Sunday between 28 August and 3 September*   136
– Proper 18: *Sunday between 4 and 10 September*   138
– Proper 19: *Sunday between 11 and 17 September*   140
– Proper 20: *Sunday between 18 and 24 September*   142
– Proper 21: *Sunday between 25 September and 1 October* 144
– Proper 22: *Sunday between 2 and 8 October*   146
– Proper 23: *Sunday between 9 and 15 October*   148
– Proper 24: *Sunday between 16 and 22 October*   150
– Proper 25: *Sunday between 23 and 29 October*   152
Bible Sunday   154
Dedication Festival: 156
    First Sunday in October or Last Sunday after Trinity   156
All Saints' Sunday   158
The Fourth Sunday before Advent: 160
    Sunday between 30 October and 5 November   160
The Third Sunday before Advent: 162
    Sunday between 6 and 12 November   162
The Second Sunday before Advent: 164
    Sunday between 13 and 19 November   164
Christ the King: 166
    Sunday between 20 and 26 November   166

Table   168
Biblical References   169
Subject Index   173

Preface

The task of the Church is unavoidably theological. As the body of Christ, we find ourselves called to explore the ways of God among men and women and, in doing so, to announce that the immediacy of the God who is Father of Jesus Christ is unqualified good news, or 'gospel'.

This theological task is carried out primarily in conversation with the documents of our faith, the Holy Scriptures. It is here that we have the earliest records of responses to Jesus and the narratives of his life which are closest to those historical events which gave rise to them. That history, of course, was never without interpretation. How could it be? Here was a story that told of God focusing the demands of his coming reign in one man; that spoke of God becoming human; that promised access to God for all who would believe that Jesus was alive again after his cruel death. Anything written of such a story was bound to include an element of interpretation along with 'bare' facts. A 'Gospel', in the technical sense, is just such a presentation of the significance of Jesus.

It is to address this reality that commentaries are written, so that those who have made it their business to study the Scriptures at some depth and length, and with some leisure to do so, may share their insights and so inform the reading of other people; they suggest possible ways of reading, not simply to instruct, but also to invite a broadening of understanding.

The decision of the General Synod of the Church of England in 1996 to adopt the *Revised Common Lectionary* for its scheme of biblical readings in public worship put it alongside a large number of other Christian denominations; it also ensured that the 'range and balance' of the biblical material that is covered is more satisfactory than has been the case in recent years; and it removed from its worship the tyranny of the 'theme', which tended to dominate interpretation of the biblical passages selected. One feature of the *Revised Common Lectionary* is its use of consecutive reading of the Bible. Such an approach cannot but help in assisting the people of God to become more keenly aware of the riches of holy scripture. If this lectionary is used sensibly in exposition and preaching, it could become a powerful tool in making Christian people more aware of how the Bible might be used in aiding discipleship.

The invitation to edit a commentary and to write a part of it was irresistible, and it has been good to look again at what we wrote three years ago and revise and expand it for this new edition. It was a particular delight to be able to undertake the task with the help of such colleagues as Georgiana Heskins and Stephen Motyer. The three of us represent different traditions within Anglicanism, but we share a love for the scriptures worked out in detailed study of them and a conviction about their status in the piety of Christian people.

We have been supported in our work by the delightful encouragement of Christine Smith, of the Canterbury Press, the patience of our families and colleagues and a great sense that what we were doing was a worthwhile project – to encourage the reading of the scriptures themselves.

MARTIN KITCHEN
Durham
Easter 2000

Introduction

On Reading St Luke's Gospel

Many who read the four Gospels probably do so with the assumption that these documents provide us with different perspectives on the life of the historical figure of Jesus of Nazareth. What may not impinge very much on our consciousness is that they are, in fact, different *versions* of the life of Jesus. It may be possible to use them to construct, with a greater or lesser degree of accuracy, a chronological account of the life of Jesus; but we need to be aware that the purpose of a written Gospel is not to furnish the reader with information about a life which lies 'beyond' or 'behind' the written record. What each evangelist wrote was the life as he knew and understood it; and therein lie the challenge and delight of biblical scholarship.

We have St Luke to thank for many of the stories which are part of Christian culture. The parables of the lost coin, the lost sheep and the prodigal son are all stories that Luke has handed down to us. From him we learn of the angels and the shepherds at the birth of Jesus, and of the road to Emmaus at the resurrection. It is he who tells of the Ascension, both in the Gospel and in the Acts of the Apostles, and it is he who, in the later volume, makes such a striking narrative of the gift of the Holy Spirit at Pentecost.

It is now commonly accepted among scholars that there exists an important level of interdependence between the first three Gospels. The fact that they can be placed alongside one another in a synopsis, so that the similarities between them can be studied, is what has given them the title 'Synoptic Gospels'. The precise relationship between them, however, is disputed. That St Mark's is the earliest is the most widely agreed conclusion, though even this is contested by some. The two Gospels of Matthew and Luke have much material in common, and an argument rages over whether the two used a common source, or one used the other. This debate becomes even more hotly contested when questions of authenticity and historicity are addressed with reference to individual paragraphs in the narrative.

In the case of Luke, we need also to remember that the Gospel which is traditionally ascribed to him is the first of a two-part work which is completed in the Acts of the Apostles. We have from him, then, an understanding of the Christian movement that takes the whole of its early history very seriously: here was something which had its origins in a Jewish past, which was centred upon the life of Jesus of Nazareth, and which continued in the story of the Christian mission begun by Peter and Paul. One commentator entitled his commentary, 'The Middle of Time'. He thus brought into focus the sense in which the story of Jesus is the mid-point between the story of the Jewish people of God and their universal counterpart, the people of God which includes the whole of humanity. Luke's broad and universal outlook is featured in the story he tells of Jesus. The good news which Jesus both preaches and embodies is inclusive and all-embracing. Outsiders, whether they are ritually impure, or foreign, or outlawed, are all included in the Kingdom of God which Jesus ushers in. Even a dying thief is told, 'Today you will be with me in paradise.'

The tradition that Luke, the companion of St Paul, was the author of the third Gospel and of the Acts of the Apostles goes back at least as far as Irenaeus in 180CE. The Gospel must have been written after Mark's, since it is dependent upon Mark, and before 130CE, because Marcion used it. Some scholars narrow this time in various ways, but we cannot be certain of any precise dating. However, we do know that Luke was a gifted storyteller; that he was committed to the life of the continuing Christian community; and that he believed in the universal nature of the gospel.

The title of the previous edition of this volume was *Word of Life*. The present work is a revised edition of that, and in order to avoid confusion with the earlier volume, this one bears the title, *Word in Our Time*. This preserves the conviction that the scriptures embody, in some sense, the Word of God to humankind. What God addresses to us is, primarily, his Son, the Word incarnate, and the scriptures, as written documents, bear witness to this primary Word. However, there is also a sense in which the written record itself may also be called 'the Word of God'. In this Gospel there is presented a particular understanding of the life of Jesus; here also begins a story of the life of the earliest Christian communities. More importantly, however, it suggests that human time is the bearer of and the witness to a Word addressed to humanity which is appropriate for 'our time'. There is an invitation implicit in the story of Jesus, which Luke makes his own by the very openness of his approach, to all who would read it to respond to the graciousness of God, who is present in the person of Jesus, and who enters time in order to bring to us a salvation which is eternal.

List of Abbreviations of Bible Translations Cited

NEB   New English Bible
NIV   New International Version
NRSV   New Revised Standard Version
RSV   Revised Standard Version

Word in Our Time

The First Sunday of Advent

Jeremiah 33:14–16; Psalm 25:1–10; 1 Thessalonians 3:9–13;
Luke 21:25–36

Advent is often treated as an advance celebration of Christmas. But nothing could be further from the truth. We begin the whole cycle of seasons and readings by concentrating not upon the first, but upon the *second* coming of Christ. Only with the readings for the fourth Advent Sunday – immediately before Christmas – do we begin to think about the incarnation.

The Sundays of Advent give us a series of readings from the prophets, concentrating on the restoration of Jerusalem, or Zion, after judgment. They are passages full of hope, beams of light in the

---

Theology

Can we still believe in a literal second coming of Christ? Many theologians would answer, 'No, not as the New Testament expects it'. Too much time has passed, and we do not inhabit the same 'apocalyptic' world-view as the New Testament writers. Yet it is important to bear in mind what the New Testament doctrine was meant to safeguard: the hope at the heart of the gospel, and with that our integrity and responsibility as human beings. We can be distracted from this by getting 'hung up' on the technicalities of Christ's return (when, where, how, and with how many trumpets, and so on), either because we want to debunk the idea or because we want to insist that it must happen literally as today's Gospel describes it. The words of Jürgen Moltmann are profound: 'From first to last . . . Christianity is eschatology, is hope, forward looking and forward moving, and therefore also revolutionizing and transforming the present. The eschatological is not one element of Christianity, but it is the medium of Christian faith as such, the key in which everything in it is set, the glow that suffuses everything here in the dawn of an expected new day' (*Theology of Hope*, SCM Press 1967, p 16).

---

darkness of sin and of God's wrath against it. Mercy shines through, grace to answer rebellion: 'I will heal them ... restore ... rebuild ... cleanse ... forgive' (Jeremiah 33:6–8) – and then Jeremiah reveals that God intends deliverance through a new king who will bring 'justice and righteousness', the answer to all the corruption and pain of the past (33:15).

Let this passage speak straight to today's world! The Church of Jesus Christ needs to speak hope into hopeless lives – the hope that derives only from *the action of God* in raising up Jesus, the Son of David, to rule in 'righteousness'. This word speaks of *relationships set right,* between people and with God, and of the *society* that results.

When will the world be like that? This longing unites people of every culture and religion. The New Testament takes this Old Testament expectation and applies it to the *new* world, the world after the coming-again of the Lord Jesus Christ. We see foretastes of it now, in the love that unites and transforms those who belong to him (1 Thessalonians 3:12–13). But really it will only come when 'the Son of Man' steps in to deliver the world from 'dissipation, drunkenness and the worries of this life' (Luke 21:34). To give up the hope of this transformation is to turn the gospel of Christ into a private, feel-good religion that finally has nothing to say about injustice and a bad world.

The Second Sunday of Advent

Baruch 5:1–9 *or* Malachi 3:1–4; *Canticle*: Benedictus;
Philippians 1:3–11; Luke 3:1–6

Today's readings follow on from last Sunday's, in that they focus on our preparation for the coming of the Lord. The passage from Malachi and the Gospel reading go together, in that the New Testament identifies John the Baptist as the 'messenger' of Malachi 3:1, sent before the Lord to prepare his way: see Matthew 11:10, Mark 1:2, Luke 7:27. We remember that John the Baptist was to 'go before the Lord, to turn the hearts of . . . the disobedient to the wisdom of the just, to make ready a people prepared for the Lord' (Luke 1:17). This picks up Malachi's expectation of a 'messenger' who will 'purify' the people, like a silversmith removing dross or a launderer removing grime, 'so that their worship may be acceptable to God' (Malachi 3:3–4).

Malachi has a particular interest in worship. In chapter 1 he attacks people for trying to fob God off with sacrifices that cost them nothing (1:8,13–14). In chapter 2 he attacks the priests for corrupt teaching and judgment (2:8–9) and for masking sexual corruption behind showy religious emotion (2:13–16). Later in chapter 3 he warns people not to cheat God in the tithes. This is all because he knows that we cannot trifle with God, particularly in worship, for a day of judgment is coming. Malachi himself was like an early John the Baptist, preparing people for the coming of the Lord.

Paul steps into the role of Malachi, in the Philippians reading. He too thinks of himself as preparing his readers to meet God: 'I'm sure that he who started this good work inside you will bring it to completion for the Day of Jesus Christ!' (Philippians 1:6). Paul is thinking of the moral transformation they need to undergo, in order to be fit to meet Christ. He prays that their love should grow, along with their perception of the truth, 'so that you may be pure and blameless on the Day of Christ' (1:10).

Is this a note that we no longer hear in today's Church? We are quick – and right – to emphasize our present journey with Christ through all the pressures and pains of life. But Advent compels us to decide what we believe about the destination of that journey; it invites us to stand in that excited crowd listening to the Baptist:

'Prepare the way of the Lord! Make his paths straight!' It is a compelling thought: the paths that Christ will tread, as he returns to this earth in glory, are those which *we* have prepared through our love for each other, for the world, and for him.

Background

Scholars have interesting discussions about the date with which Luke begins our gospel reading. The fifteenth year of Emperor Tiberius brings us probably to 28CE (emperors' 'years' were measured differently in different places). It looks as though John was preaching for over a year before Jesus appeared, for John 2:20 gives a date of 30 or 31CE for this incident soon after the start of Jesus' ministry. The best date for the crucifixion (based on calendrical calculations conducted by Professor Colin Humphreys of Cambridge University) is April 33CE.

The Third Sunday of Advent

Zephaniah 3:14–20; *Canticle*: Isaiah 12:2–6; Philippians 4:4–7;
Luke 3:7–18

John the Baptist was a prophet. That is to say, when he spoke,
people felt themselves to be addressed directly by God. His words
carried tremendous power – or, to use an old expression, 'convicted'
those who listened. Even hardened 'sinners', like tax-collectors and
Roman soldiers, were suddenly willing to change their lives in
response to his preaching (Luke 3:12–14). God himself was present
in the words of his prophet – the God who, the prophet said, was
'coming soon' with the awful fire of judgment to burn away all fruitless branches and chaff from his harvest.

'Hellfire preaching' is now a thing of the past. But John the Baptist
would caution us: make sure that you retain the truth of God as
Judge, even if you reject the style in which that truth was communicated by some of your forefathers! Human justice is always inade-
quate. The guilty are acquitted, the innocent suffer, the murderers
and rapists remain free. Is that the end of the story? John the Baptist
was fired with prophetic passion that there is an ultimate court
before which we must all must render account. Life is not meaning-
less. Actions (and inactions) ultimately matter. God sees all, and will
judge all . . . and so we must repent.

Should we relate to God, then, just as a fearful Judge? Our
Philippians reading tells a very different story. There 'the Lord is
near' does not strike terror, but causes *rejoicing*. It puts an end to
worry (4:6), rather than causing it! Because 'the Lord is near', his
peace may guard our hearts in all circumstances.

What makes the difference? The answer is in the last phrase of the
reading: 'in Christ Jesus'. We are only able truly to appreciate the
headline 'Rejoice in the Lord always!' if we read the dramatic story
underneath: the story that tells how, when Jesus came, John the
Baptist was disappointed that the judgment failed to arrive as
expected. He sent to ask Jesus, 'Are you the one who is to come, or
should we wait for another?' (Matthew 11:3). And Jesus replied not
in terms of judgment, but of mercy to the weak – using the words of
another prophet, Isaiah (Matthew 11:4–5, see Isaiah 35:5, 61:1).
God had more in mind than just judging the wicked.

The interplay between judgment and mercy is the constant theme of the prophets. Zephaniah illustrates it for us today. His prophecy begins with words of judgment more powerful than any others in the Old Testament, looking forward to 'the day of the Lord's wrath', when 'in the fire of his passion the whole world will be consumed; for a full, terrible end he will make of all the inhabitants of the earth' (Zephanaiah 1:18). So speaks God's justice in the face of the vile corruption he sees. But his *mercy* speaks another language, as we see from our reading, with which Zephaniah's prophecy ends: a bubbling celebration of the love and *nearness* of the Lord, who has set aside disaster and judgment, and brought Zion into security and festival.

Theology

The relationship between judgment and mercy prompts questions. Can they fit together into one comprehensive picture of God, or are they incompatible elements of the presentation of God in the Bible? Professor Walter Brueggemann, in his *Theology of the Old Testament* (Fortress Press, 1997), emphasizes their incompatibility in the Old Testament. He finds them expressed alongside each other in the famous text, Exodus 34:6–7: 'The Lord, the Lord, a God merciful and gracious . . . forgiving iniquity and transgression and sin, yet by no means clearing the guilty, but visiting the iniquity of the parents upon the children . . .'. The Lord both forgives and does not clear iniquity – and Brueggemann points out that Israel never knew for sure which side of the character of their God they would encounter. Judgment and mercy existed in an uneasy truce. Saul was judged and rejected for his sin, but David was forgiven and restored.

Within the theology of the Bible as a whole, the New Testament resolves this tension by the incarnation, death and resurrection of Christ. 'God was in Christ, reconciling the world to himself, not counting our sins against us,' wrote Paul (2 Corinthians 5:19). Theologians debate the precise mechanism of the atonement – how is it achieved by the life, death and resurrection of Christ? But it is clear that here judgment and mercy find resolution, as God himself acts to defuse the power of our rebellion, to absorb sin and death into himself in Christ, so that they 'count' no more.

The Fourth Sunday of Advent

Micah 5:2–5a; *Canticle*: Magnificat *or* Psalm 80:1–7;
Hebrews 10:5–10; Luke 1:39–45 *or* 39–55

As a newly-ordained curate I took a group of students to lead a service in a local old people's home. We included the Magnificat, Mary's Song, in the service. Afterwards I was shocked when one of the residents objected strongly to this ancient song of thankfulness at the birth of the Saviour. 'It's just not true!' he complained. 'Knocked the powerful off their thrones? Fed the hungry? Raised the weak? We don't see God doing that!' My newly-ordained theology had no answer.

What *is* the answer? We blithely include Micah's prophecy in the list of those fulfilled by the coming of Jesus, because it names the place of his birth (Micah 5:2, see Matthew 2:3–6). But what about the rest of the prophecy: 'He shall stand and feed his flock . . . they shall live secure, for now he shall be great to the ends of the earth; and he shall be the one of peace' (5:4–5)? Has this been fulfilled?

This question takes us to the heart of the Advent message. The Saviour will enter the world not as a mighty deliverer, but as a fragile baby. God prepares a body for him, so Hebrews tells us (Hebrews 10:5), not an army to wage war against injustice. A single human body, ready to do God's will (Hebrews 10:7): that is God's answer to human corruption, because corruption needs to be dealt with on a spiritual, and not just on a social, level. This body will offer itself as the full and final sacrifice to achieve 'holiness' or 'sanctification' (Hebrews 10:10) for all who will seek salvation through him. The temptation is always to offer our own sacrifices – to attempt to meet our needs, and the needs of the world around us, by *our* means, to *our* agenda, through *our* campaign. And there's nothing wrong with trying to put the world to rights! Politicians the world over are animated by the desire to leave the world a better place. But in the long run politics comes to ruin on the hard rock of human wickedness – that is, our wickedness, which makes *us* the proud who need to be dethroned and the selfish rich who are sent empty away.

Mary's Song anticipates a great concern for social justice in Luke's Gospel. He loves to display Jesus' action on behalf of the poor, the

8

sick, the rejected, the insignificant. But when he moves on to Part Two of his story, in the Acts of the Apostles, he does not show the Church campaigning for social justice as part of its response to Christ. Rather, he loves to point to the changed character in which the power of the good news is seen. New love, new patience, new boldness, new joy and wisdom, all through the power and presence of the Spirit in the community of the risen Christ – this is what will

---

Text

The quotation of Psalm 40:6–8 in Hebrews 10:5–7 is intriguing. The author of Hebrews takes the phrase 'a body you have prepared for me' as spoken *by Christ* about *the incarnation*. But a quick glance at Psalm 40 reveals (a) that verse 6 does not mention 'a body' (NRSV: 'you have given me an open ear'; NIV: 'my ears you have pierced'); and (b) that the Psalm is not by or about the Messiah, but is a prayer for rescue from trouble.

The answer to puzzle (a) is not difficult: the author of Hebrews is quoting from the Septuagint, the Greek translation of the Old Testament made in the second century BC, which takes a stab at a difficult piece of Hebrew and translates it 'you prepared a body for me'. But puzzle (b) is more difficult. This is a Psalm 'of David' (see the heading), and the first part of the Psalm (verses 1–10) is about the proper way of expressing thankfulness to God for all his goodness. The verses quoted in Hebrews make the revolutionary point that extravagant temple offerings and sacrifices are *not* the way. Rather, God looks for exact listening, and perfect obedience, to his will. (Verse 7 should probably be translated 'in the roll of the book I have been given instruction' – referring to the Law.)

The author of Hebrews often applies Psalms of David to Jesus, usually because they say things about David which could not have been true of him, or of any king of Israel, and therefore must point forward to someone of whom they *are* true. In this case, the point seems to be that no one, actually, can truthfully claim to do the will of God. We all, including David, fall short. But Jesus does not. And since the author of Hebrews was reading the Septuagint, he found other hints that this passage was really only true of him – especially 'you prepared a body for me'.

'turn the world upside down', even when the powerful try to oppose it (Acts 17:6).

And of course we know that he will only 'be great to the ends of the earth' (Micah 5:4) when this process is complete, crowned by his second Advent to claim his world for himself.

Christmas Eve

2 Samuel 7:1–5,8–11,16; Psalm 89:2,21–27; Acts 13:16–26;
Luke 1:67–79

As we prepare for the Festival of the Incarnation, the lectionary directs us to a string of passages which together reflect on Jesus as 'Son of David'. This is of course one of his titles in the Gospels (see, for example, Matthew 9:27, 12:23, 20:30f), and was a regular title for the Messiah among the Jewish rabbis. But what does it mean?

The foundational passage is 2 Samuel 7. Here, when David desires to build God a 'house' (a temple in Jerusalem), God responds through the prophet Nathan that, instead, he will build a 'house' for David – that is, a royal dynasty. He promises that he will 'raise up' a son for David, and 'will establish the throne of his kingdom forever' (2 Samuel 7:13), bringing him into a unique father–son relationship with himself (2 Samuel 7:14). Through the rule of this line of kings, Israel will be protected and secure from all threats (2 Samuel 7:10–11).

But this promise was not fulfilled! Psalm 89 bewails its non-fulfilment, in the later part from which no selection is taken for today. It is important, however, to be aware of it. After celebrating the 2 Samuel 7 promise in glowing terms, the Psalm continues, 'But now you have spurned and rejected him; you are full of wrath against your anointed. You have renounced the covenant with your servant; you have defiled his crown in the dust . . . Lord, where is your steadfast love of old, which by your faithfulness you swore to David?' (verses 38–39,49).

The *problem* was the destruction of Jerusalem by the Babylonians in 587 BC. At that point the last Davidic king was carried off into exile, his sons were executed (2 Kings 25:7), and the unbroken line of four hundred years ended. The Davidic kingship was never restored in Jerusalem after the exile. So it is not surprising to find the prophets turning this failed promise into an expectation – of a coming Davidic king who will enjoy that father–son relationship with God, and under whose rule Israel will be rescued from all her enemies, both external and internal (her sin), and dwell secure among the nations (see, for example, Jeremiah 23:5; Ezekiel 34:23; Hosea 3:5; Zechariah 12:8).

Against this background we can understand the emphasis in the New Testament on Jesus as son of David. Matthew announces this right at the start of his Gospel (1:1), and builds his opening genealogy around it. The line has not died out! Luke underlines it several times in his birth narrative: 1:27,32; 2:4,11, and especially in Zechariah's song which forms the Gospel today. The line of David is being restored (verse 69), as the prophets foretold (verse 70), to protect and deliver Israel from all her enemies (verses 71,74f).

God had more surprises in store! In fact Luke traces the further development in his two-volume work, the Gospel and the Acts: from this very 'Jewish' beginning, in which Jesus appears just as the Davidic Saviour of Israel, the scope gradually widens until the *whole world* comes under the potential rule of this King . . . as the prophets foretold! (Isaiah 9:7, 55:3–5; Psalm 2:6–9).

Christmas Day

First set of readings

Isaiah 9:2–7; Psalm 96; Titus 2:11–14; Luke 2:1–14 *or* 1–20

The three sets of readings for Christmas Day develop three complementary themes. The first set broadly coheres around the theme of the grace of God; the second around the holy people whom God calls into being through Christ; and the third around the presence of God among his people. There are other themes in all three sets, of course, but these form a thread through each.

'The grace of God' summarizes the whole significance of Christmas in Titus 2:11: 'The grace of God has appeared, bringing salvation to all.' The biblical word 'grace' has a technical meaning completely different from its modern meaning, and yet all except two of the many recent translations retain 'grace' in Titus 2:11. The exceptions are the *Contemporary English Version*, which paraphrases with 'how kind God is', and the *Christian Community Bible*, which has 'his loving plan'. The inadequacy of these alternatives explains why the other versions have kept the unfamiliar word 'grace'.

What does it mean? The Hebrew *chesed* and the Greek *charis* are used particularly of God, and refer both to his attitude and to his action. They express the attitude of love and commitment which impels God to *act* to save his people, however undeserving they may be. So, frequently, 'grace' refers to an event, in and through which God's attitude of love and compassion is revealed because we see him acting to rescue the lost. Thus grace can 'appear', as in Titus 2:11.

This is exactly what the beautiful Isaiah reading expresses. Like its modern counterpart, ancient Israel was surrounded by enemies, bristling with armies and threats. Into this fear breaks the 'gracious' promise of God – of a child through whom a universal rule of peace will be established, a new 'David', a 'Prince of Peace' who will reign over all, and for ever. Whereas 'the boots of the tramping warriors' (verse 5) sound a threatening drumbeat of pillage and destruction, the Lord 'gives' a son, and with this son light (verse 2), joy (verse 3), freedom (verses 4–5), and peace (verse 7).

'Peace' is the angels' theme in Luke 2:14. From a biblical perspective, *peace* is the world's greatest need, because alienation is its greatest problem: alienation from its Creator, between its races, in its streets and in the hearts of its people. To be able to speak peace realistically to this distracted world, and to hearts torn with pain, is the angels' great privilege – and ours too, as we take that same song, and message, onto our lips at this time. To us, too, a Saviour has been born, a child under whose rule peace will grow. And (say the angels) this is all for 'the people he favours' – not an exclusivist description, as though there are people whom he does *not* favour, but a way of describing humankind. We are 'the people he favours', towards whom his grace *appears* in Christ.

Theology

These readings raise the issue of the fulfilment of prophecy. In what sense is it right to speak of Old Testament prophecy being fulfilled through the birth of Christ?

Some treat the prophecies like almanac predictions which have come true: Jesus' birth of a virgin (Isaiah 7:14) in Bethlehem (Micah 5:2), heralded by a star and kings (Isaiah 60:1–3). But this is not fair to the prophecies. Undoubtedly, neither Isaiah nor Micah had a figure like Jesus in mind. They were both thinking of a king in the line of David – perhaps a super-David, who would truly represent God (Isaiah 9:6) and his rule (Isaiah 9:7), and of course would be born in Bethlehem, the town of David. It is unlikely (though not impossible) that Isaiah was thinking of a virgin birth in 7:14.

Some scholars have swung to the opposite end of the spectrum in arguing that there is fundamentally no connection between these prophecies and the birth of Christ, except in 'the eye of the beholder', that is, in the convictions of the first Christians. According to this view, the first believers forged a connection between these prophetic texts and a set of events which actually did not match them at all (and we could mention other prophecies and aspects of Jesus' life here, especially his death and resurrection to which the New Testament applies Psalms 2, 16, 22 and 69, Isaiah 53, Zechariah 11–13, and so on). But this view runs so counter to the whole tradition of the Christian use of the Old Testament – on which our lectionary rests! – that many have hesitated to endorse it.

Is there a middle way, between the 'almanac' approach and its opposite? The great German scholar Gerhard von Rad proposed 'typology' as a way forward. He suggested that we should think of the Bible as a continuing story, in which the earlier stages prefigure, but do not pre-tell, the later. On this view, the prophecies are not like the preview of the Chelsea Flower Show, admitting the privileged (and the press) to an earlier experience of the whole thing, but rather like *Pygmalion* to *My Fair Lady*, or the 'Peelers' to the Metropolitan Police, or like the Athenian Assembly to the United States Senate, or like Michelangelo's sketches in relation to their full painted versions – prefigurings whose main lines and principles are later developed into a much fuller expression which both builds upon and transcends the original.

This approach seems to work!

Christmas Day

Second set of readings

Isaiah 62:6–12; Psalm 97; Titus 3:4–7; Luke 2:8–20 *or* 1–20

The restoration of Jerusalem is a vital theme in the later prophets who lived through or ministered after its destruction by the Babylonians. The theology of (for example) Psalm 46 was deeply shaken by that awful trauma in 587BC: 'God is in the midst of the city, it shall not be moved.' Yet not only was the city 'moved' – horribly – by Nebuchadnezzar's army, but the prophets were convinced that God had abandoned it (for example, in Ezekiel chapters 8–11). Jerusalem could only be destroyed, because he was no longer 'in the midst'.

Was it possible to make sense of this disaster? The prophets explained it thus: (a) God has done this, not the Babylonians, because (b) his people Israel had sinned deeply against him; but (c) his grace will not permit him finally to abandon Israel, and so (d) Israel will be made holy, delivered from this fatal sinfulness, and as a token of this (e) Jerusalem will one day be restored, and the Lord will return to dwell there again.

This explains the ideas that come together in our Isaiah reading today. The watchmen on the walls of Jerusalem are looking for the return of the Lord – this theme is taken up in the next chapter, Isaiah 63. When he comes, he will restore the city (verse 7), but the centre-piece of that restoration is the bringing back of 'the people' (verse 10), who will be called 'The Holy People, the Redeemed of the Lord' (verse 12). So the Lord comes supremely as 'Saviour from sin' (verse 11), rather than just as 'Rebuilder of Jerusalem'.

The theme of the creation of a holy people holds together the New Testament and Gospel readings also. In Titus 3 we are reminded that the whole point of God's action as 'Saviour' (verse 4) is so that we might be reborn and renewed by the Holy Spirit (verse 5). And in Luke 2 this is the hidden significance of the shepherds as primary actors in the drama of the Saviour's birth. They epitomize Israel's need for salvation. Shepherds were outcasts in first-century Jewish society – symbols of Israel's dislocation and uncleanness. Strict Pharisaic standards ruled that shepherds were unclean, because they wandered across other people's land, could not keep the sabbath properly, engaged in trade with Gentiles, and were suspected of pilfering and of keeping unclean animals (pigs) as well. Some Pharisees forbade the buying of wool, milk or kids from wandering shepherds. It speaks volumes that it was to such people that the angelic message was first communicated: (a) they are associated with the rest of Israel ('to you in the city of David'); (b) they vividly symbolize the re-creation of Israel at the heart of this Saviour's task; and (c) they become the first missionaries to their fellow-Jews (verses 17–18), a wonderful reversal illustrating Luke 4:18, 6:20–21 and 13:30. If shepherds are the focus of this Saviour's work, then this will be salvation indeed!

Background

The role of the shepherds in Luke's birth narrative anticipates one of the vital themes of his Gospel – Jesus' ministry to the outcast and the marginalized. Whether it is shepherds, or Samaritans, or lepers, or women, or prostitutes, or wealthy tax-collectors, Luke loves to show Jesus breaking down the social barriers which distanced such people from Israel's core identity. We learn about the social and religious significance of Jesus' actions – and of the shepherds' true role in the Christmas story – from the rabbinic lists of 'despised trades' which were held to be incompatible with full obedience to the Torah. In the list in the later tractate 'Sanhedrin' in the Babylonian Talmud (25b) 'herdsmen' appear with gamblers, usurers and tax-collectors as people who could not be admitted as witnesses in court: all the more remarkable, therefore, that the shepherds are the first witnesses of the Saviour's birth.

Christmas Day

Third set of readings

Isaiah 52:7–10; Psalm 98; Hebrews 1:1–4 *or* 1–12; John 1:1–14

In Anglican churches this set of readings must be used at some point on Christmas Eve or Christmas Day each year. The readings from Hebrews and John were set for Christmas Day in the *Book of Common Prayer,* and before that in the widely-used *Sarum Missal,* so for many centuries Christmas has been viewed through the lens of these texts. What do they reveal?

They form a close-up lens that peers through the outward elements of the story – the parents, the places, the politics – and gives us sight of the inner dynamic, the heart, of this event. Isaiah 52:7–10 is a well-chosen companion, for it expresses the belief, still deeply felt in the first century, that God himself would come to Israel as Saviour and Deliverer, when the Day of the Kingdom arrived. Against this background, Hebrews 1 and John 1 assert the fulfilment of that expectation, and explain how it has happened.

Both texts draw deeply upon the 'wisdom' tradition in Jewish thinking. For some details about this, see the comment on the readings for the Second Sunday of Christmas below. Setting the two passages alongside each other, we observe four elements in common between them:

(1) *Jesus is actually called 'God'.* This is rather rare in the New Testament, but it is clearly the intention in Hebrews 1:8 and in John 1:1. It fits with the language used elsewhere in both passages: for instance, 'he is the reflection of God's glory and the exact imprint of God's very being' (Hebrews 1:3, NRSV) – here the usual word 'reflection' means literally 'outshining' and pictures the light that streams from a light-source. And in John 1:14 again the word 'glory' is used, reminding readers of the glory of *God* which inhabited the temple, and which now is to be seen in God's *Son.*

(2) *Jesus is presented as a Revealer.* In John he is 'the Word', about whom John the Baptist – representing the whole prophetic tradition – testifies. Through the prophets the light shines (1:5), but they are not the light themselves (1:8), unlike the Word through

whom the glory of God shines directly. Similarly Hebrews 1:1–2 contrasts the prophetic revelation with God's speaking through 'a Son', although Hebrews uses the Old Testament as 'testimony' to Jesus throughout its chapters.

(3) *Jesus is the Agent of Creation.* This follows on from the points (1) and (2), because God's *speaking* and *creating* are closely related, as we see in the dramatic and repeated 'and God said' of Genesis 1. But in Hebrews 1:2–3 it is *the Son* 'through whom' God created, and who 'sustains all things by his powerful word'. Similarly through 'the Word' of John 1:3 'all things came into being'. When he speaks, he speaks the words of God (compare John 12:49; 17:8), and these have life-giving, creative power.

(4) *Jesus comes as the Saviour from Sin.* Hebrews 1:4 slips in an unexpected reference to 'purification of sins' as an aspect of the *creative* work of the Son. Just as he 'makes' the world (1:2), so he 'makes' purification (the same Greek verb is used). In John the equivalent notion is that of 'becoming children of God' (1:12). The Son comes to create something wonderfully new – the possibility of a wholly new, purified relationship with God in which we too can call him 'Father'.

Text

The famous phrase 'full of grace and truth' in John 1:14 illustrates the testimony of the prophets to Jesus. For, as many scholars now recognize, it is the equivalent in Greek of the Hebrew phrase often translated 'steadfast love and faithfulness', which is quite frequent in the Psalms (57:3; 86:15; 115:1; 138:2, for example), and which appears in Exodus 34:6, a passage which seems to 'lurk' behind John 1:14–18. There Moses, the greatest of the prophets, asks to see God; but in line with John 1:18 he is only allowed to hear the name of God being proclaimed: 'The Lord, the Lord, a God merciful and gracious, slow to anger, and abounding in steadfast love and faithfulness . . .'. So whereas Moses mediated the law to Israel (John 1:17), and was allowed to proclaim God's nature as 'full of grace and truth', that 'grace and truth' has actually come into being through Jesus Christ, because he is 'full' of it (John 1:14, 17).

The First Sunday of Christmas

1 Samuel 2:18–20, 26; Psalm 148; Colossians 3:12–17;
Luke 2:41–52

These passages fall into two pairs. Psalm 148 and Colossians 3 encapsulate a response of praise and thankfulness to God for the gift of his Son. The Psalm invites us to join a shout of adoration rising from the whole of creation, prompted by the reason given in the last verse: 'He has raised up a horn for his people . . .'. 'Horn' symbolizes strength, security, a champion leader – as in Zechariah's song in Luke 1:69. So because God has acted to rescue his people, the whole of creation is invited to join in worship. We find the same thought in Romans 8:18–25 and Revelation 5:6–14. In Colossians 3 the note of praise is amplified by a response of lifestyle. With unique clarity this passage sums up the quality of Christian life which enables us to live in joyful harmony with God, with each other, and with creation – animated by one hundred per cent loyalty to the Lord Jesus. Reflection on Psalm 148 and Colossians 3 will enable us to see how worship, our identity as human beings within creation, and our character and lifestyle are all tied up together.

The other two passages take the Christmas story further by pointing us to the childhood of Christ. Some of the later 'apocryphal' Gospels – like the Infancy Gospel of Thomas, the most famous of them – attempt to fill the gap in our knowledge by telling stories about Jesus' childhood that make him old before his time, describing extraordinary miracles performed by him, and wonderfully wise sayings. But this single incident told by Luke is so much more realistic. It shows Jesus acting with all the thoughtlessness and over-the-top enthusiasm displayed by twelve-year-olds the world over – but at the same time, *within* that thoughtlessness and passion, a consciousness of a special relationship with his 'Father'.

Mary has every reason to object to Jesus' behaviour. At twelve he could be expected to know when Passover ends, and what are the arrangements for the journey home. His parents were trusting him to behave 'sensibly'. If he had wanted to stay longer, he should have asked them – and doubtless they would have agreed. But *so great is his passion* for the temple, and for the discussions of the Torah held there, that all these 'sensible' considerations are driven from his mind, and he even sleeps two further nights there. Jesus finds himself gripped by a driving awareness of God, an overwhelming sense of God's presence in the temple, and a deep desire to think, speak and act within that relationship. He cannot tear himself away! His parents don't 'understand' (verse 50), not because they cannot make sense of his words, but because they cannot relate to such a strong sense of attachment. Jesus realizes that he has another 'Father' who is not looking for him (verse 48), but who has found him, captured him, made him at home in the temple.

This story does not just reveal something about Jesus' humanity and spirituality, nor does it simply challenge us over our assumptions about the 'spiritual' capacity of children, but it asks us to seek the same overwhelming, passionate commitment to God which may drive 'prudence' out of the window for us, too.

Text

The sources and historicity of the birth narratives are of course hotly debated by scholars. A widely-held view is that the differences between the Matthean and Lukan stories are so great that they cannot be harmonized, and must be regarded as largely legendary. The 'supernatural' elements of the stories (especially the appearances of angels in both Gospels) are taken to support this view, especially since the Infancy Gospels show the desire to elaborate supernatural stories about Jesus' birth and childhood.

On the other hand, the differences between the canonical and apocryphal Gospels are immediately obvious. The 'supernatural' elements in Matthew and Luke are actually muted in comparison. Both Matthew and Luke have an interest in the fulfilment of scripture which is absent from the others. They are not impossible to harmonize with each other, and Luke seems almost explicitly to cite Mary as his source (Luke 2:19,51), while Joseph is the dominant character in the Matthean birth narrative. Ultimately, our presuppositions about the historical interest of the Gospels play a formative role in the conclusions we reach on questions like these.

The Second Sunday of Christmas

Jeremiah 31:7–14 *with* Psalm 147:17–20 *or* Ecclesiasticus 24:1–12
with Wisdom of Solomon 10:15–21; Ephesians 1:3–14;
John 1:10–18 *or* 1–18

The beautiful Jeremiah passage sets the scene for the first set of
alternatives today. We meet the Israelites on the road back from
exile to their home, rejoicing not just in the fact of homecoming but
in what has made it possible – the new, restored relationship with
their God. 'I have become a father to Israel,' he declares, 'and
Ephraim is my first-born' (verse 9), and so the road home opens
before them.

But they carry their sorrow with them. I wish that the reading
extended to include one more verse, Jeremiah 31:15: 'Thus says the
Lord: "A voice is heard in Ramah, lamentation and bitter weeping.
Rachel is weeping for her children; she refuses to be comforted
for her children, because they are no more."' (NRSV). Because
of the joy of homecoming, there is an agony of regret over all who
have been lost, and who cannot know this joy with them.

This is the verse quoted by Matthew with reference to the 'slaugh-
ter of the innocents' by Herod, at the time of Jesus' birth (Matthew
2:16–18). The presence of that little story in Matthew 2 is a puzzle.
Does it not seem deeply incongruous, that the birth of the Saviour
should actually *cause* such suffering? But actually it is the birth of the
Saviour which *shows up* that incident in its true horror, just as it is
the homecoming which makes more dreadful the loss of those who
cannot share it. The 'innocents' of Bethlehem are not mere statistics,
further anonymous notches on a tyrant's sword, lost to history, their
blood swallowed by the earth, like the death of so many others in our
world. Alongside Jesus' birth, their death is truly horrible – because
he is the Saviour, and because we know that ultimately he will not
escape death at a tyrant's hand. He too will be swept away by fright-
ful injustice, but his death will be the means of life and of homecoming for all who belong to him.

Ultimately he, not Israel, is the one over whom God says 'he is my
firstborn' (Jeremiah 31:9; John 1:14), and then he gives the right to
become children of God, to all who receive him (John 1:12). At the
heart of today's Gospel reading is the reference to the rejection of the

Word (verse 11): he too is not able to come home, as he wishes, to 'his own', but is turned away. And at the heart of our New Testament reading from Ephesians 1 is the tiny reference to his 'blood' by which we have been redeemed from our sins (verse 7). He stands alongside all the fallen, all those deprived of homeland, all those lost in sin and swallowed by death, so that through *his* death they might receive a homecoming, new life, membership of the family of God.

The other set of readings, involving Ecclesiasticus and the Wisdom of Solomon, requires us to think about the Jewish 'wisdom' tradition and its relevance for our understanding of Jesus. On this, see the *theology* box that accompanies this comment.

Theology

The 'wisdom' tradition, exemplified in Sirach (Ecclesiasticus) 24, was Israel's way of coping with the 'problem of transcendence'. This is a problem that faces all theistic belief-systems, that is, religions or philosophies that assert the existence of a supreme deity. The question is: does this deity act within the world, and if so, how? This question was felt particularly sharply in the ancient world, because the Greek philosophical tradition tended to regard the matter of the world around us as either intrinsically evil or at the least incompatible with the divine. How, then, can there be any contact between God and the world?

The doctrine of creation helped the Old Testament to overcome this 'problem of transcendence': for if God was involved with the world when making it, then presumably he can continue to act within it. But then the little difficulty of *sin* rears its ugly head: how can God in his absolute holiness remain in contact with a sinful world? The tabernacle, pointedly known as the 'tent of meeting' (for example Exodus 33:7), gave the answer of the Old Testament: God takes up residence in the middle of his chosen people, but they can only actually 'meet' him through an elaborate system of sacrifices, and even then he remains in splendid isolation in the 'Most Holy Place' at the centre of the tabernacle. In any case, how real is this thought of God 'dwelling' in a tent or building? Dedicating the Jerusalem Temple, Solomon hit the nail on the head: God is supposed to inhabit the Temple, but 'will God indeed dwell on the earth? Even heaven and the highest heaven cannot contain you, much less this house that I have built!' (1 Kings 8:27).

Enter 'the wisdom of God'. If God himself remains aloof, his wisdom need not. In Sirach 24 God's 'wisdom' is pictured as acting independently of God himself, 'coming forth' from God (verse 3), 'seeking' a resting place on earth (verse 7), then 'commanded' by God to 'make your dwelling in Jacob' (verse 8), particularly in the Temple in Jerusalem (verses 10–11). Later in the chapter, this 'wisdom' of God is identified with the book of the Law of God, Israel's most prized expression of God's presence in her midst (Sirach 24:23).

'Make your dwelling in Jacob' (Sirach 24:8): here the same unusual Greek word is used as in John 1:14, 'the Word became flesh and dwelt among us.' Like wisdom, God's Word comes from him, and seeks a dwelling, coming to 'his own' (verse 11), but finding a resting place not in Israel generally but only among 'those who believed in his name' (verse 12). In the most dramatic way possible, the problem of transcendence is tackled by asserting the incarnation of the wisdom of God. God is present now, not through some vague quality ('wisdom') expressed in a book, but in a person of flesh and blood who is his 'Word', that is, his very mind and heart expressed into human form and speech, and living 'among us' so that we can 'behold his glory' (verse 14). What a message!

The Epiphany

Isaiah 60:1–6; Psalm 72:10–15 *or* 1–15; Ephesians 3:1–12;
Matthew 2:1–12

Setting the Isaiah and Ephesians passages alongside each other reveals a problem. For in Ephesians Paul seems to say that he has just discovered, by special revelation, what Isaiah long knew about – that 'the Gentiles have become fellow-heirs' (3:6). Isaiah clearly speaks of the 'ingathering' of the Gentiles, who (in his picture) come in droves to Jerusalem, bringing 'gold and frankincense' and seeking to 'proclaim the praise of the Lord' (60:6). In what sense did Paul feel that he had just discovered this well-known idea? For actually this expectation of universal blessing is commonplace in the Old Testament, especially in Isaiah. This expectation of course underlies the story of the Magi, coming with those very gifts 'to the brightness of [his] dawn' (Isaiah 60:3).

The answer lies in the shape of the expectation. For Isaiah the expectation is centripetal; for Paul it is centrifugal (terms used by Professor Joachim Jeremias in discussing this issue). Isaiah expected that the Gentiles would come to Israel, drawn towards the centre because of the blessing poured out there, and thus would be incorporated into Israel's relationship with God. With this expectation, the Jews never developed a substantial missionary movement. But Paul, on the other hand, realized that God had something greater in mind. It was not inappropriate to say that God was bringing Gentiles in, to join Israel, and Paul says this clearly in Romans 11:17–24. But it would be fuller, and truer, to say that God was calling both Jews and Gentiles to join something new, the Church of Jesus Christ, and in order to spread this invitation God was sending out missionaries, like himself, hurled out centrifugally from Jerusalem into the rest of the world, to summon Jews and Gentiles together into the household of God in Christ. Paul of course thought that he himself had been especially commissioned for the Gentile half of this missionary operation, and we can see in Ephesians 3:8–10 how essential he believed this out-going ministry to be.

Because their movement is centripetal, seeking out the new King, the Magi symbolize for us the result, but not the method, of Christian mission. Christians belong to a worldwide fellowship in which all barriers of race and culture have been broken down. I believe that this is what Paul has in mind in Ephesians 3:10 when he writes of 'the manifold wisdom of God' being made known through the Church to 'the rulers and authorities in the heavenly places'. One of the significances of these 'rulers and authorities' (see the *Theology* box below) was as the 'guardian angels' of particular nations. So the multinational Church of Jesus Christ, in which Jews, Gentiles (Greeks, Turks, Serbs, Albanians, Tutsi, Hutu) are united in one

Theology

The Pauline references to 'rulers and powers' (see also Ephesians 1:21; 6:12; Colossians 1:16; 2:10,15; Galatians 4:8–9; Romans 8:38; 13:1–3; 1 Corinthians 2:6–8) have been the centre of a fascinating recent discussion. To what does Paul refer by these terms? A survey of the references reveals the breadth of association in his mind. These terms can refer to human, political power (Romans 13; 1 Corinthians 2) or, at the opposite end of the spectrum, to the devil and his minions (Ephesians 6). In between we are puzzled to discover that they were created in, through and for Christ (Colossians 1), while also constituting the enemies which strive to separate us from the love of Christ (Romans 8) and which were defeated at the cross (Colossians 2). Does Paul use these terms without any consistent meaning, or is there a united reference which holds them together?

Professor Walter Wink, of Auburn Theological Seminary, New York, has written extensively on this, and has proposed a way of viewing 'the powers' which holds together the ambivalence of Paul's references. The powers, he suggests, are the inner essence of human organizations or movements, that implicit quality which we label when we call an international corporation 'greedy', or a culture 'decadent', or a people-group 'friendly', or a crowd 'hostile'. So 'authorities', body through the cross (Ephesians 2:16), proclaims by its very being that these guardian angels have been put out of a job.

Epiphany thus faces us with some sobering questions: is this really the message displayed by the Church of Jesus Christ, at the beginning of the twenty-first century? How do we rate our performance, in *showing* that these 'angels of the nations' have received their redundancy notices?

Wink suggests, can be both visible (governments) and invisible (the inner 'quality' of governments).

Wink's view works well when we think of the 'powers' that actually shape and determine people's lives. All of us, whether we like it or not, are prey to social, political, environmental, economic, ideological and psychological forces beyond our control. Many of these have an 'outer' and an 'inner' aspect, as for instance in the case of a government which, for social and ideological reasons, prefers to wage war with a neighbour rather than feed its own population in a time of famine. To believe that Christ has been raised supreme over all such powers (Ephesians 1:20–21) is encouraging indeed!

But Wink's view does not work so well when we set it alongside Paul's manifest conviction that there really exist 'cosmic powers of this present darkness . . . spiritual forces of evil in the heavenly places' (Ephesians 6:12). In Paul's case we should perhaps think of a sliding scale of 'power', from satanic beings, to more neutral kinds of angels, to human manifestations of various kinds of evil power manifested through vile ideologies or economic injustice or natural disasters (perhaps inspired by spiritual evil), to actual human governments who receive their power from God (Romans 13) but can misuse it. Whatever powers we face, however, none of them can separate us from the love of Christ (Romans 8:38–39)!

The Baptism of Christ

The First Sunday of Epiphany

Isaiah 43:1–7; Psalm 29; Acts 8:14–17; Luke 3:15–17,21–22

It is something of a commonplace to say that, in his baptism, Jesus associates himself with people at their point of need. Here is a great crowd of Jews ('all the people', Luke says, 3:21) 'convicted' of their need of forgiveness by this extremely charismatic preacher, John the Baptist, whom they even think may be the Messiah (3:15). 'No, I'm not!' says John. 'When the Messiah comes he will baptize you with the Holy Spirit and with fire, not with water.' It is a real surprise, therefore, when the Messiah appears, and does not baptize anyone, whether with water, Spirit or fire. Instead, he submits to John's water-baptism, and himself receives the Spirit. In order to *be* the one who baptizes with the Spirit, he must first stand among 'all the people', associating himself with their prayer for forgiveness and restoration, and be anointed for the ministry through which *he* will be the means of answering that prayer.

The Isaiah and Acts readings add an extra dimension to this thought of Jesus' association with us. In Isaiah we discover that the same images of water and fire can be used of the threats and sufferings of life which seem to stop us from achieving restoration and new life. The images in Isaiah 43:2 represent all the dangers that threaten God's people on their journey back to Jerusalem. 'They cannot stop you!' Isaiah assures the people in God's name.

We can apply this thought powerfully to the water of baptism. Water is essential for life, but it is also a very dangerous medium. It washes, but it can also destroy, sweep away, drown. In our baptism, therefore, we do not just enact the washing away of sin. We also face our death, symbolically, and associate it with the death of Christ in whom death becomes the gateway to eternal life. And with our death we also face our struggles and sufferings, the waters that threaten to swamp us, all the little anticipations of our death which punctuate our lives. Baptism says to us: Jesus the Saviour stands alongside you in each of those experiences, for the water through which he passed symbolized that for him, too. It is not surprising that, when Jesus refers to his 'baptism' later in

Luke's Gospel, it is his death which he has in mind (Luke 12:50).

What of the fire of the Spirit? Why is this image associated with the Holy Spirit, when 'fire' too, in Isaiah, suggests the life-threatening dangers through which travellers must pass? Fire is associated also with the presence of God (Exodus 19:18, for example), and with sacrifice (Leviticus 1:7), and with purging (Numbers 31:23; Isaiah 4:4). And when the Spirit of God comes upon us, as upon the Samaritans in Acts 8, then the trials that we fear become means of cleansing, ways in which the Holy Spirit makes us holy, able to experience the presence of God and to make sacrifices of love and worship that are pleasing to him. Whether it's water or fire through which we pass, our baptism in water and fire unites us with the Christ who turns suffering and death into means of life for us.

The Second Sunday of Epiphany

Isaiah 62:1–5; Psalm 36:5–10; 1 Corinthians 12:1–11; John 2:1–11

'For as a young man marries a young woman, so shall your builder marry you' (Isaiah 62:5, NRSV). The NRSV rightly notes that the Masoretic text (the original Hebrew with vowel-points added) has 'your sons' rather than 'your builder', and this is the translation preferred by the *New International Version*. The translation 'your builder', however, only involves a change in the vowel-points, not in the basic letters of the Hebrew text, and is surely correct. It fits with the second, explanatory, half of the verse: 'As the bridegroom rejoices over the bride, so shall your God rejoice over you.'

So the verse involves a wonderful mixed metaphor. The builder becomes the bridegroom. Or, as Paul puts it, 'In Christ the whole structure is joined together and grows into a holy temple in the Lord; in whom you also are being built together into a dwelling-place for God in the Spirit' (Ephesians 2:21–22). Here the metaphor is a little less mixed: God builds the Church in Christ so that he may then occupy it by the Spirit.

The Old Testament passages concerned with the rebuilding of Jerusalem, or of the temple, are frequently applied to the Church in the New Testament. As we saw above (see the comment on the second set of readings for Christmas Day, where the second half of Isaiah 62 is prescribed), the central idea in this element of Old Testament expectation is not the rebuilding of the city, but the moral and spiritual restoration of God's people, to right fellowship with him and with each other. And that brings us to our New Testament reading, the first of a series of three from 1 Corinthians 12–13: for in this famous section on 'spiritual gifts' – which includes 1 Corinthians 14 also – the notion of 'building' or 'upbuilding' is central for Paul. He does not actually use this word until 14:3, but it expresses a vital principle which underlies chapters 12 and 13 also: spiritual 'gifts' are not gifts to the individuals who receive them, but to the Church as a whole, because through their exercise the whole 'body' of the Church is to be 'built up'. This notion of the 'building' of the Church by the Lord, through the distribution of spiritual 'gifts', draws upon the tradition of the rebuilding of Jerusalem to be a fit place for the Lord himself to occupy. The Church is to be the company of the redeemed!

It is well worth reflecting on the complete unclericalism of Paul's picture in 1 Corinthians 12. Some of these 'spiritual gifts' are compatible with occupying an 'office' in the Church, but Paul does not mention this, emphasizing rather the direct role of the Holy Spirit in 'distributing' or 'activating' the gifts (verse 11). Nor does Paul seem to care about the gender of the recipients. It is the newness of it all that excites him: the Holy Spirit himself is active, rebuilding the people of God, leading them in love and worship, speaking to them, enabling them to serve each other and the world around.

This newness is also the theme of the Gentile reading, in an interestingly complementary way. The stone jars of water represent what Judaism offers to those who need purity. Jesus takes that water and transforms it – as a token of what he will do next: go to the temple in Jerusalem and 'cleanse' it, to signify its rebuilding through his resurrection (John 2:13–22). Everything is being rebuilt, transformed, mended, in today's readings!

The Third Sunday of Epiphany

Nehemiah 8:1–3,5–6,8–10; Psalm 19; 1 Corinthians 12:12–31a;
Luke 4:14–21

The Sundays of Epiphany focus and reflect on the incidents
through which Jesus was 'revealed' to those who first encoun-
tered him. Following the initial focus on the Magi, we look at his
baptism (the first Sunday), and reflect on the way in which baptism
turns us into a pilgrim people for whom the hardships of the journey
are moments of growth; then we focus on Jesus' first 'sign', through
which his disciples began to believe (John 2:11, the second Sunday),
and we reflect on the rebuilding of God's people which this signifies;
next (today) we turn to the report of Jesus' sermon in the synagogue
in Nazareth, and we are prompted to reflect on the role of the scriptures in revealing Jesus. Finally, on the fourth Sunday, we turn to the
story of Jesus' presentation in the temple, and reflect on the pain and
the cost of love.

The story of Ezra reading the law to the people of Jerusalem is
moving and evocative. Their attentiveness to it arises from their
experience of seeing God at work: in a remarkable way, against all
odds, Jerusalem has been rebuilt, and they know that God has been
with them. But the effectiveness of the reading depends upon careful
presentation (in an open, public place, standing on a platform, and
using many assistants) and clear interpretation (Ezra's assistants
make sure that the people understand the application of the law to
themselves). The impact of this reading becomes clear in the following chapters: confession of sin (Nehemiah 9) and a new commitment
to serve God (Nehemiah 10).

It looks as though this remarkable movement under Ezra and his
army of lay assistants was the first time that principles of interpretation had been formulated to enable old laws to speak with fresh relevance to the present. Without interpretation, the word of God
remains dead, addressed to a bygone age. The task of the preacher
and teacher is just as vital today: by every means possible, to impress
the contemporary power of the scriptures upon modern (and post-
modern) ears.

Jesus does exactly this in the Nazareth sermon with which
Luke begins the account of his ministry. His first recorded public

words are those of Isaiah 61:1–2, with the remarkable commentary: 'Today this Scripture has been fulfilled in your hearing' (verse 21). In other words, Jesus claims that he alone has the right to use a real 'first person' when reading this text. For every other reader, the words are those of someone else. This speaks powerfully of Jesus' self-consciousness and of the way in which the scriptures shaped both his sense of call and the interpretation of his ministry by others. He acts out Isaiah 61, with its two-pronged programme

Text

This quotation from Isaiah 61 plays a significant role in Luke's Gospel. Luke advances this story, of Jesus' rejection in Nazareth, from its position in Mark's order (Mark 6:1–6), so that it sits at the head of Jesus' public ministry, and so that Isaiah 61:1–2 forms a kind of interpretative 'grid' through which to read the events which follow. There are significant allusions to the same passage later in the Gospel (for example, 6:20–21; 7:22; compare Acts 10:38), and the themes of the quotation fit with Luke's emphasis on Jesus' ministry to the poor, the weak and the socially marginalized. Whether it's poor shepherds (2:8ff), a rich tax-collector (19:1–10; 18:9–14), an apostate-waster (15:11ff), unclean Samaritans (17:11–19; 10:29ff), a prostitute (7:36ff), a crucified terrorist (23:39–43), or even just *women* (for example, 7:11ff; 8:1–3; 13:10–17), Luke loves to show the doors of the Kingdom being thrown wide for them, in line with this programmatic proclamation on Jesus' lips at the start of the story.

Isaiah 61:1–2 is a messianic text, and thus appropriately applied to Jesus, granted the confession of Jesus as Messiah! But we see Luke's creative engagement with the scriptures, and notice something important about his way of interpreting them, as we ask which came first: Jesus, or Isaiah 61? Chronologically, the answer is clear. And the prior existence of Isaiah 61 doubtless helped Luke and others to identify *Jesus* as the Messiah. But then in turn the story of Jesus' ministry shaped their reading of Isaiah 61. Exactly the same *interplay* between text and experience takes place for us today – and is actually vital to the process of biblical interpretation, enabling the scriptures to be the living Word of God for us, too.

of preaching and healing for the poor, and then Luke uses Isaiah 61 to help us understand who Jesus is.

These readings call us to stop and reflect on the role of the scriptures in our lives. Do we live out of them in the way exemplified by Ezra, by Jesus and by Luke?

The Fourth Sunday of Epiphany

Ezekiel 43:27–44:4; Psalm 48; 1 Corinthians 13:1–13; Luke 2:22–40

The Ezekiel passage needs some explanation! This comes from the final, 'apocalyptic' section of Ezekiel which centres around the reconstruction, in vision, of the Jerusalem temple. Ezekiel lived through the destruction of the temple by the Babylonians in 587BCE, and was commissioned (in part) to tell his fellow-Jews that this awful event took place because the Lord had abandoned the temple, driven to leave by the corrupt worship there (Ezekiel 8–11). But destruction and disaster are never the end of the story with God. Even at the moment of his departure, God gives a promise of restoration (11:17–20). And so in chapters 40–48 Ezekiel describes the restoration in detail, involving not just the reconstruction of the sanctuary but the renewal of the people and their worship.

Ezekiel is conducted around this visionary temple by an angelic guide (the 'he' of 44:1 – described in 40:3–4), and sees the Lord returning to the temple, through the east gate (43:1–5). Now in 44:1–3 we read that, following the Lord's entry there, only 'the prince' will be allowed to use that gate. 'The prince' is the messianic figure described (for instance) in Ezekiel 37:24–28 – the coming Davidic king who will exercise a restored kingship over a restored land and people.

All this helps us to understand the 'consolation of Israel' or the 'redemption of Jerusalem' for which Simeon and Anna, and many like them, were longing (Luke 2:25,38). Many took the view that the Herods were not the restored kingship, and that the massive temple in Jerusalem, under construction by Herod the Great at the time of Jesus' birth, was not the fulfilment of Ezekiel's vision. Simeon and Anna were such – longing for the fulfilment of this prophetic vision, consumed with desire to see worship restored, the people redeemed, God glorified – and the Prince on the throne. They live with the agony of the tension between vision and reality: the vision of what will be, the reality of what is. And, surprisingly, this agony is not dispelled as Simeon holds the baby Prince in his arms, assured by the Spirit that it is 'He'. For himself, a gentle departure in peace (2:29); but for Mary, a sword through the heart (2:35).

This is the agony that always accompanies the love of God. The more we love him, the more we will feel the inadequacy of all other experiences, and the more pain we will feel at the state of the world, and of our churches, and of our neighbours. In our consecutive reading of 1 Corinthians 12–13 we set Paul's beautiful hymn about love alongside the story of Simeon and Anna. And they illustrate the pain of love – the pain hidden underneath words like 'patient', 'not irritable', 'bears all things', 'endures all things' (1 Corinthians 13:4,5,7). The love that Paul describes can bear anything, because it has its eyes fixed not on earthly circumstances but on God himself, longing for the moment when we will 'know fully, even as we have been fully known' (verse 12) – the moment of consolation, of redemption, when worship will be perfect and God truly glorified!

In this longing we stand beside Simeon and Anna, and rejoice in the birth of the Prince who assures us that such love is not illusory. Through the suffering love of his people, this Prince will be revealed to the world.

The Presentation of Christ

Malachi 3:1–5; Psalm 24:7–10 *or* 1–10; Hebrews 2:14–18;
Luke 2:22–40

Our Psalm and Old Testament reading set the scene by pointing to the coming of the Lord to Zion as background to the Gospel story of the presentation of the infant Jesus in the temple in Jerusalem. Luke makes Jesus' appearance in the temple so significant, greeted with profound words of prophecy, that we can well believe this tradition is in his mind. At last the promise has been fulfilled, and the Lord's Christ has appeared in the temple, the 'messenger of the covenant' (Malachi 3:1) who brings cleansing to Israel and light to the Gentiles (Luke 2:32).

But he comes as a baby, not as a conquering warrior. Did Simeon and Anna expect this? They might have picked up hints from passages like Isaiah 9:2–7, but general Jewish expectation was that the Messiah would suddenly appear, as if from nowhere, to deliver his people and establish the Kingdom of God. That is what Malachi led people to expect – a 'sudden' appearance in the temple, to sweep away all impurity in a torrent of fire. Who can endure it? Other prophecies pictured the Lord as a mighty warrior, advancing on Jerusalem with irresistible force (for example, Isaiah 63:1ff).

In contrast to this expectation, we are presented with such frailty: the frailty of the baby, and of his two elderly welcomers. Luke subtly underlines the theological point involved here in his introduction to the story in 2:22–24, by alluding there to three Old Testament themes, which underline the 'baby-ness' of Jesus most movingly: the ritual of purification (verse 22a), the redemption of the first-born (verse 23), and the presentation to the Lord (verse 22b). For some details on these, see the *Background* box. Like every other Jewish baby, Jesus has made his mother 'unclean' by the process of child-birth, and she needs to be purified. And like every other Jewish first-born male, Jesus must be 'redeemed' because he is 'holy to the Lord'.

But wait: in Jesus' case this means much more than for other male babies. We already know of the very special sense in which he is 'holy to the Lord' (Luke 1:35). And so, thirdly, unlike every other Jewish baby, Mary and Joseph take their first-born to the temple to 'present him to the Lord', re-enacting Hannah's presentation of

Samuel to the sanctuary at Shiloh (1 Samuel 1). They give him back *to* the Lord, because he is a unique gift from the Lord, and from now on he 'belongs' in the temple (thus we are prepared for the next story in Luke 2 – verses 41–52).

So the reality of Jesus' humanity is powerfully pictured here: not a mighty warrior, but an ordinary – and yet extraordinary – baby. As the author of Hebrews puts it, 'Since the children share flesh and blood, he himself likewise shared the same things' – so that he might fulfil a unique role as Saviour from sin and death (Hebrews 2:14). He steps into the muddy waters of our physicality, with all its capacity for stain, and smear, and weakness, so that we might be saved.

So it is deeply appropriate that he should be greeted by two of the frailest members of the worshipping community in the temple: and that they should be the ones anointed by the Spirit to recognize him.

Background

The regulations for purification after childbirth are given in Leviticus 2:1–8. The process of childbirth was held to make women ritually impure for forty days. At the end of this period mothers had to present themselves at the sanctuary, to offer the sacrifice noted by Luke here (verse 24) – which, incidentally, was the sacrifice prescribed for poor families.

In 2:23 Luke quotes one of the regulations concerning the redemption of the first-born male, Exodus 13:2. Here God claims all first-born males for himself. The first-born of every cow, sheep or goat had to be sacrificed, symbolizing God's possession (Numbers 18:7), but first-born human beings had to be 'redeemed' with a money-offering (Numbers 18:15–16; see also Exodus 13:12–13). The fact that there is no mention of a money-offering by Joseph and Mary underlines the thought that they are 'presenting' Jesus to the Lord in that special, further sense – the complete dedication of his person and life to God, like Samuel, for the unique role and ministry God intends.

Ordinary Time – Proper 1

Sunday between 3 and 9 February

Isaiah 6:1–8 *or* 1–13; Psalm 138; 1 Corinthians 15:1–11;
Luke 5:1–11

The calendar changes gear at this point. We leave behind the
Christmas season, and move into 'Ordinary Time'. So we begin
some more consecutive readings in the period before Lent, focusing
on Luke's Gospel (the prescribed Gospel for Year C), and on 1
Corinthians 15. As always, the Old Testament readings are chosen to
match the Gospel passage.

However, it is often the case that united themes hold together all
three readings and the Psalm, and this is the case today. The theme is
'call to ministry'. In reflecting on this we must bear in mind the point
Paul has emphatically made in 1 Corinthians 12–14, the section leading up to today's reading: that we are all called to ministry by virtue
of our baptism (see especially 1 Corinthians 12:7–13). 'Ministry' is
not a special calling given to a chosen few. Some may be called to
special ministries, but that is different!

Isaiah and Peter were ordinary guys, until the day one set off for
the temple, and the other sat down on the beach to mend his nets. A
day like any other . . . except that *that* was the day God stepped in.
The settings, and the events, could hardly be more different, but the
effect and its *cause* were the same: they came face-to-face with God,
their lives were turned upside down, and they received a whole new
direction and an impossible task to fulfil.

In Isaiah's case it was a unique visionary encounter, absolutely
overwhelming in its power. He sees the hem of God's robe, gains an
awesome sense of his holiness and greatness towering above him,
hears the heavenly attendants flitting around the temple and singing,
senses that the temple is about to burst, unable to contain such glory
(verse 4), suddenly feels deeply convicted of his sinfulness, experiences a dramatic cleansing with a burning coal pressed to his mouth
– and in spite of all this cannot resist offering himself when God
seems to need another missionary (verse 8).

In Peter's case it involved listening to the strange yet gripping
teaching of this young rabbi, allowing his boat to be used, and then

agreeing – for some reason – to get the nets dirty again even though he had just cleaned them after a fruitless night's work. Though he must have been impressed already by Jesus, nothing prepared him for the staggering event which then had him, too, on his knees confessing his sin and receiving an invitation not just to lend his boat but to join Jesus on the platform, netting crowds for the Kingdom.

Paul also felt completely unworthy. 'I am unfit to be called an apostle,' he complains (1 Corinthians 15:9). And yet, like Isaiah and Peter, 'by the grace of God' (1 Corinthians 15:10), he could look back on a ministry in which he had been faithful to the gospel he was called to proclaim. He reminds the Corinthians of its importance (verses 1–2), summarizes its content (verses 3–4), emphasizes its foundations (verses 5–9), and celebrates its power (verses 10–11).

Paul would have been quick to sing Psalm 138, looking back on his experience in ministry. And so may we all, whatever ministry we have received within the Church of Jesus Christ.

Ordinary Time – Proper 2

Sunday between 10 and 16 February

Jeremiah 17:5–10; Psalm 1; 1 Corinthians 15:12–20; Luke 6:17–26

'The secret of true happiness' – like the elixir of youth and the gold of Eldorado – this is the 'hidden grail', in search for which we humans bend all our efforts, even when we dress up the search as something more respectable. And here it is! The scriptural definition: true happiness is living in the Truth, whatever your circumstances.

Contrasted 'blessings' and 'curses' hold together the Psalm, Jeremiah 17 and the Gospel reading. And in 1 Corinthians 15:12–20 Paul tells us that the most wretched of all existences would be to base your life on the 'fact' of the resurrection of Christ, only to discover that this was a lie. The Psalm and Jeremiah tell us that true 'blessedness' (that is, prosperity, ultimate human well-being) depends on whom you trust: to whom you relate yourself, in dependence for the sustenance of your life. If you trust in others ('mere mortals', Jeremiah 15:5) or in 'the advice of the wicked' (Psalm 1:1), then your life will shrivel and die. But if you trust in the Lord (Jeremiah 15:7) and in his self-revelation (Psalm 1:2), then your life will be a green and fruitful tree even 'in the year of drought' (Jeremiah 15:85, Psalm 1:3).

'Even in the year of drought': this is the thought that brings us into Luke 6:17–26. Jesus is surrounded by the most amazing crowd, a terrible gathering of human need, some of whom have travelled fifty miles or more to bring their sick for healing (verses 17–19). In the midst of all this need Jesus addresses his disciples (who form a large proportion of the crowd), and pronounces the 'blessedness' of the poor, the hungry, the grief-stricken and the persecuted. Then, in exactly balancing contrast, he pronounces 'woes' upon the rich, the satisfied, the jolly and the idolized.

It is important to define exactly the sense in which 'blessedness' is ascribed to the poor, and 'woe' to the rich. In contrast to the belief of some, it is not poverty in itself which is a blessing – no more than riches in themselves are a 'woe'. This would be nonsensical. We can get the right sense if we paraphrase: 'You are blessed even when you are poor, for the Kingdom of God is yours; you are blessed even in your present hunger, for you will be satisfied; you are blessed even in your present grief, for you will laugh.' This paraphrase enables us to see that the 'blessedness', the secret of true happiness, consists in the fact that, for Jesus' disciples, present suffering is sure to be followed by a great reversal.

So here, too, happiness does not consist in what you have, but whom you know. It does not depend on present prosperity, but on living in relationship with Jesus who promises future laughter. In other words, we humans have an inescapably eschatological aspect to our being: our identity is defined not by our present but by our

Theology

1 Corinthians 15:12 poses a puzzle: how can members of the Corinthian Church deny the resurrection of the dead? Is this not such a foundational article of Christian faith that those who deny it have effectively posted their resignation?

This question takes us right to the heart of a modern debate. Is denial of the resurrection compatible with Christian believing? In the popular debate which surrounded the views of Dr David Jenkins, the former Bishop of Durham, this question quickly generated another: is it possible to deny the bodily resurrection of Christ, and continue to believe in his resurrection, or his 'aliveness' to us today? Jenkins' answer to this question was, of course, a resounding 'Yes'. Our experience of the living Christ today, he argues, does not depend upon an emptied tomb in Jerusalem in 33CE.

To the question in this second form, 1 Corinthians 15:12 is highly relevant. For the denial of the resurrection in Corinth was not a denial of life after death (virtually everyone believed in that, in the first century), so neither was it a denial of the continued life of Christ after death, nor (in all likelihood) of the possibility of spiritual access to Christ in his post-mortem existence. Rather, it was a denial of the bodily resurrection of Christ, on the grounds of a fundamental dualism of body and spirit which argued that true resurrection means separating the spirit from the body that hampers and defiles it. On this (very Greek) understanding of the human person, Christ's resurrection must have been a resurrection just of the spirit, leaving the body firmly behind.

future, and in relationship with Jesus that future is 'blessed' indeed.

Is this realistic? This is where 1 Corinthians 15:12–20 comes in! Paul makes it crystal clear: if Christ has not been raised from the dead, as the token of the final 'resurrection of the dead', then 'your faith is futile, you are still in your sins, and, what's more, dead Christians have been lost completely' (verses 17–18). The truth of the resurrection of Jesus (verse 20) is the ultimate foundation of a 'blessed' life, provided we have our roots sunk deep into him (Jeremiah 17:8).

This Paul will not accept – not chiefly because the 'empty tomb' is part of the historical tradition he transmits (he doesn't mention the empty tomb in 15:3–8), but rather because this view of resurrection rests upon an impossible anthropology, in his view. There is much evidence in his writing that he simply did not work with this Greek dualism in his fundamental thinking about human beings. We are 'monistic' entities – that is, body–spirit units that cannot suffer the loss of any part of ourselves without dreadful damage to us as people, beings in which spirit and body are so intertwined that a spiritual-and-not-bodily resurrection is simply impossible.

I believe that this would be Paul's reaction to the debate surrounding Dr David Jenkins' views on the resurrection of Christ. He would disagree, not with Jenkins' view of Christ, but with the underlying anthropology which allows Jenkins to posit Christ's 'aliveness' today without a bodily resurrection in 33CE. The Greek anthropology, which Paul rejects, regarded death as a release, a freeing of the soul from the shackles of physicality. But for Paul death is an enemy – albeit 'the last enemy', whose days are now numbered (1 Corinthians 15:26) – because it assaults what we are as human beings, tears us apart, ruins us. That is why we weep in the face of death, and should not take refuge, I believe, in illusory talk about merely passing through a curtain to 'the other side'. Only in Christ is this dreadful enemy overcome.

This of course raises questions about the relation between body and spirit in death and resurrection, which Paul himself tackles later in 1 Corinthians 15, which is to be read next week.

Ordinary Time – Proper 3

Sunday between 17 and 23 February

Genesis 45:3–11,15; Psalm 37:1–11,39–40;
1 Corinthians 15:35–38,42–50; Luke 6:27–38

Love for enemies is the most distinctive way in which the ethical teaching of Jesus departs from other codes of behaviour, both Greek and Jewish (in his day), and of course from contemporary non-Christian ethics, whether religious or not. Its very distinctiveness makes it difficult to understand and apply. Jesus makes it very practical in verses 28–30, but can he really mean it? These rules seem to undermine social justice. If we applied them in the law courts, justice would be turned on its head.

So perhaps 'rules' is the wrong word to describe the practical applications with which Jesus illustrates the principle in verses 28–30. Dr Robert Tannehill calls them 'focal instances' rather than 'rules': the idea, he says, is that these are instances of the way in which love for enemies might be focused in practice. It might mean going so far as to give away your shirt to an enemy, and giving to every beggar you meet. Because they are not rules, they do not make it mandatory that we must give to every beggar. In fact, it might be a better expression of love not to give, under certain circumstances. But these 'focal instances' press the application to an extreme, to show how important the principle is, and how uncompromising our adherence to it must be.

The principle arises, of course, from the nature of God himself, as Jesus says in verse 35. This view of God is slightly in tension with the picture of him as the God of Israel, who has chosen a special people for himself. This is why we find a very different saying in the Dead Sea Scrolls, where the *Community Rule* of the Qumran Community opens with a statement of their fundamental principles: that 'they may love all the sons of light, each according to his lot in God's design, and hate all the sons of darkness, each according to his guilt in God's vengeance.' Their attitude to outsiders was likewise patterned on what they took to be God's attitude – one of vengeance and hatred. But because Jesus' God shows equal kindness to all (with verse 35, compare Matthew 5:45), even to those who hate him, so must we.

44

This even goes beyond the Old Testament. We find moving instances of forgiveness, as in today's reading of the climax of the Joseph story in Genesis. Instead of being filled with bitterness towards his brothers for the years of hardship caused by their hatred of him, Joseph forgives them and emphasizes that God, rather than they, had engineered his move to Egypt, for their sake! Such love is God-given, and life-creating, and brings music out of discord in the muddle of human relationships. It cuts through the prickliness and hurt with a wonderful 'It doesn't matter!' which embraces and reconciles the offender, prizing love over vengeance. But Joseph is loving family, not enemy. Only in Jesus do we find the love which lays down its life for those who hate the lover. But that is the love by which we sinners have been embraced in him (see Romans 5:8–10), and which creates not just new joy now, but a resurrection life beyond the grave.

Some comment on our third reading from 1 Corinthians 15 is provided in the *Theology* box below. The beautiful final section of 1 Corinthians 15, verses 51–58, is not prescribed for the Principal Service at any point in the *Revised Common Lectionary*, and so it might well be added today!

Theology

We continue our reflections on Paul's resurrection theology, in response to the series of readings from 1 Corinthians 15. Throughout this chapter, his monistic anthropology is a core presupposition from which Paul works. In 15:35 he imagines the question, 'How are the dead raised? With what kind of body do they come?' This is not an innocent request for enlightenment, but a scornful objection to Paul's insistence on *bodily* resurrection. It means: 'How can you talk about resurrection of the dead? What kind of body can be resuscitated after it has decayed in the tomb, perhaps for many years?' This imaginary objector thinks that a monistic anthropology requires the resuscitation of corpses, a manifestly ridiculous idea.

Paul rejects this, and proposes a much more subtle way of holding together person, body and spirit in death and resurrection. He agrees that 'flesh and blood cannot inherit the Kingdom of heaven' (15:50), but does not conclude from this that we must leave 'flesh' behind in order to enter the presence of God: for there are many different kinds of flesh (15:39–41), and it is God's intention, through the death and disintegration of our present 'flesh', to generate a new kind of 'body', a 'spiritual body' (15:44), which will 'bear the image of the man of heaven' (15:49), so that we can 'put on immortality' (15:54). The image of the dying seed is crucial for Paul (15:37) – an image that he probably gained from Jesus himself (John 12:24): for Jesus is supremely the seed that dies, so that much fruit may be born. In 1 Corinthians 15 the vital thought is of our union with Christ, so that his experience of death and resurrection becomes ours. It is 'in Christ' that all are made alive (15:22), and it is only 'those who belong to him' (15:23) who can regard him as the 'firstfruits' of their own resurrection.

Paul says nothing beyond his 'seed–plant' analogy to envisage how the body of the resurrection might be related to our present, physical bodies. Nor does he make any comment about the apparent time lag between physical death and final resurrection. These are questions which tease the imagination. At the least we must say that Paul presents us with a mode of existence which, while in continuity with our present life, is very different in form. And he himself believed that on death he would 'be with Christ' (Philippians 1:23), even if it must be in what C. S. Lewis called 'Lenten lands', where we will 'fast in naked spirituality' before 'we shall return and re-assume the wealth we laid down' with the gift of a body which enables us to be ourselves, with all the memories and relationships that make us what we are, in the new environment of the New Creation. (C. S. Lewis, *Letters to Malcolm: Chiefly on Prayer*, Collins, 1964, pp 123–4)

The Second Sunday before Lent

Genesis 2:4b-9,15–25; Psalm 65; Revelation 4; Luke 8:22–25

At the time of writing our television screens are once again show-ing scenes of starvation in east Africa – dead cattle signalling economic disaster for people already starving, children's puzzled eyes staring out of emaciated bodies, the result of three years' drought.

Our readings today celebrate God as Creator: a glorious convic-tion, easy to celebrate while standing in the landscape conjured up by Psalm 65. But what about the current landscape of east Africa? Or any other scene in which lives are carried away by drought, flood or earthquake?

This question is not foreign to today's readings. In our Gospel reading the disciples are faced with the potential, immediate loss of their lives in a freak Galilean storm. It only takes one, big wave . . . and a near miss becomes another headline, another grieving family. The image of Jesus sleeping in the midst of this storm is powerful indeed. What does it convey?

The point of the story is not just his power to quell the storm, evoking Psalm 65:7 and God's power to still 'the tumult of the peoples'. Throughout the Bible, the surging of the sea is a picture of the powers of evil and chaos, reflected in war and turmoil between people.

Nor is the point his rapid response to the disciples' desperate prayer, encouraging though this is. We too may find our storms immediately quelled as we turn to an apparently sleeping Lord in wobbly faith. But of course the storm may still rage, even though we pray. The story provides no assurance of sudden deliverance from desperation.

So the chief point of the story lies in its sense that the desperate prayer, and Jesus' dramatic response, were a second-best, the result of doubt and fear rather than of faith – so that it would have been better if the disciples had remained as 'oblivious' to the storm as Jesus, mentally 'asleep' to it even as they struggled with the oars and the balers, confident in God's rule and provision for them.

Is this realistic? To that question the only answer faith can give is 'Yes – of course!' Faith does not just look in sorrow at the parched fields of northern Kenya, but sees through them, discerning the

Father who mantles the hills of Europe and America with grain, perceiving the God who breathes his breath into us, so that *only in relationship with him* do our lives have significance and sustenance (Genesis 2:7), and sharing the vision of John the Seer, who saw the sea of chaos and evil solidified into crystal before the throne, and the whole of creation obedient to its Creator (Revelation 4).

It speaks volumes that some of the contemporary (first-century) Jewish apocalypses picture the four 'living creatures' of Revelation 4:6–8 as in conflict with each other even in heaven, reflecting the conflicts and chaos between these representatives of creation on earth. But in Revelation there is no conflict, only united praise of 'the Lord God the Almighty'. The same question – is this realistic? Ultimately, it can only be realistic because Revelation 4 is followed by Revelation 5, picturing the way in which 'the Lamb' has shared all our sufferings, and through his death has ransomed us so that we can serve God on the earth (Revelation 5:9–10), however awful our circumstances.

The Sunday Next before Lent

Exodus 34:29–35; Psalm 99; 2 Corinthians 3:12–4:2; Luke 9:28–36
or 28–43

The readings before we enter Lent prepare us by focusing our thoughts on the glory of Christ revealed in the transfiguration – that glory which will now be veiled, symbolically, through Lent, as we focus on his sufferings for us.

Just as the glory of Christ was veiled through his ministry – so that the three disciples were completely overwhelmed by this amazing, unusual incident – so his glory is veiled in the world today. We are part of the crowd at the bottom of the mountain (Luke 9:37), among whom his healing power is experienced, but only with pain and difficulty. It would be possible for us to be jealous of Moses, who got so close to God that his face shone with reflected glory. Not for us! We are part of the outside crowd there, too, standing outside the 'tent of meeting', wondering what is the quality of that experience, of actually speaking with God face-to-face.

But there is something very surprising about St Paul's handling of the transfiguration story in 2 Corinthians 3. We expect, naturally, that Jesus Christ will be the equivalent of Moses, the one who shines with the glory of God because of his closeness to him. After all, Moses and Elijah appear with Jesus on the mountain, the two greatest Old Testament prophets, because they were both figures around whom the glory of God shone (with Exodus 34, compare 2 Kings 2:11). But Paul does not do this. First he compares himself to Moses, as we see from the beginning and end of the reading. Whereas Moses veiled the glory of God, so that the people could not see it clearly, on the contrary 'by the open statement of the truth we commend ourselves to the conscience of everyone in the sight of God' (4:2). This contrast in favour of himself is the burden of the whole passage from 3:4 onwards – Paul actually calls Moses a minister of 'death' and of 'condemnation', because he simply gave laws to obey, in contrast to his own ministry which is 'of the Spirit' and 'of justification' (3:7–9).

The underlying rationale for this extraordinary denigration of Moses appears in 3:15–18, and is truly staggering in its boldness. It is not Jesus Christ who is the equivalent of Moses, but 'all of us, who with unveiled faces behold the glory of the Lord'. We do not stand outside, but are like Moses when he went back into the tent of meeting (Exodus 34:34). This is because 'where the Spirit of the Lord is, there is freedom' (3:17), freedom from the incapacity to recognize, receive and reflect the glory of God. Like Moses in the presence of God, 'we are being transformed from one degree of glory to another. This comes from the Lord who is the Spirit!' (3:18).

What sort of 'seeing' of the glory of God does Paul have in mind?

Text

Paul uses two rather disputed words in 2 Corinthians 3. Some translations use the word 'fading' with reference to the glory in verse 13 (RSV, NIV, for example), as though Moses veiled his face to stop the Israelites from seeing that the glory was slowly fading from it. This translation is not wholly impossible, but it is now recognized that it does not do justice to the word that Paul uses, which does not mean 'fade'. His expression is rather obscure, it has to be said, but the NRSV (margin) probably captures it more accurately: '. . . to keep the people of Israel from gazing at the end of what was being set aside'. This whole way of approaching God, through a prophetic mediator, is being set aside. Here 'end' can mean 'termination' but probably (so suggests Professor Richard Hays) it means 'supreme expression of': in the case of Moses we see the supreme expression of a way of approaching God which is now being set aside because of Christ and the Spirit given through him.

In verse 18 Paul uses another vivid word which is equally difficult to translate. 'Seeing . . . as though reflected in a mirror' (NRSV) represents one Greek word, which is also translated as 'reflect' (NIV), 'reflect as in a mirror' (NEB), 'behold' (RSV), 'contemplate' (NIV margin). The word is based on the Greek word for 'mirror', but here the question is: are we the mirror, reflecting the glory of God like Moses, or are we looking at the mirror? And if the latter, is the mirror each other, in whom we see God's glory reflected, or is it Jesus Christ? Scholarly opinions differ. In the light of the parallel between us and Moses, which is fundamental to Paul's thought here, the simple translation 'reflect' is probably the best.

He explains further a few verses later: 'It is the God who said, "Let light shine out of darkness," who has shone in our hearts to give the light of the knowledge of the glory of God in the face of Jesus Christ' (2 Corinthians 4:6). He has in mind a spiritual apprehension of Christ, a Spirit-given confession that God's glory is to be seen in him – and of course seen in him not primarily on the mount of the transfiguration but on the cross, in the valley, touching an agonized father and his tortured son. To see the glory of God there is to enter the tent of meeting with Moses.

And so we enter Lent, looking for the glory of God in the face of our suffering Lord Jesus Christ.

Ash Wednesday

Joel 2:1–2,12–17 *or* Isaiah 58:1–12; Psalm 51:1–17;
2 Corinthians 5:20b-6:10; Matthew 6:1–6,16–20 or John 8:1–11

Hypocrites are those who play-act. Religious people who feign 'goodness' may be said to have robbed God of the praise due to him. The readings at the beginning of the season of Lent call us to take off our costumes and our greasepaint and to make changes in the way we live. We are to take a long hard look at who we have become, without make-up, so that in our turning towards Good Friday and Easter, it will be the goodness of God (rather than something phoney and less durable) which earths and energizes our journey.

The prophet Joel uses a plague of locusts as a dire warning of the judgment that will follow if the people do not change their ways. This may be a cryptic reference to the physical invasion of Israel. More likely the locusts are a device, symbolizing national disintegration, borrowed from the prophet Amos. They reiterate, in the fourth century BCE, a much older prophetic message: repentance and prayer is the price of the Lord's continual toleration of a recalcitrant people. The oracle comes from a period of peaceful coexistence between religion and Persian domination, and the prophet alerts his contemporaries to the perennial danger of allowing an alien culture to set the agenda for God's people.

The reading from Isaiah is more specific. The practical needs of the post-exilic community provide the context for a call for justice for the hungry and the homeless. The emptiness of religious observance shows a wrong attitude towards God, who cannot be confined to any human institution. Both Joel and Isaiah warn us of the superficiality which can distort and enfeeble discipleship.

Whereas for Joel 'the day of the Lord' is a once-for-all and terrifying event in the future, for Paul it has already dawned. Jesus, God's anointed one, makes every day a day of salvation – a day in which to respond to God and to be grounded in the grace of God. Writing to the Corinthians, he tackles the thorny question of how to behave properly as Christian people – without play-acting. He reminds them that human inadequacy can block the transmission of grace, but insists that his own energy and perseverance in the face of difficulties

52

are recognizable signs that he embodies 'the life of Jesus' (4:10–11). Tribulation strips off our theatrical garb and enables the life of faith to be lived at a deeper level.

Almsgiving, prayer and fasting – three signs of a religious person – are all opportunities for 'play-acting' according to our Gospel passage from Matthew. Applause is the actor's reward and is not a proper goal for those whose 'piety' should be directed solely towards God. The quest for public recognition, appropriate to an entertainer perhaps, can never be the motivation for Christian disciples. They depend on the forgiveness of God and must receive that in a direct relationship with him, unalloyed by any limelight for themselves. The resources for faith lie in knowing ourselves loved and accepted, warts and all, by God alone. Such was the experience of the woman in John 8; and she stands as the symbol of the forgiven, like all the rest of us.

Interpretation

'The early Church continued the Jewish custom of linking fasting and prayer, and in the lives of the saints the two almost always go together.' (Oxford Dictionary of the Christian Church, 3rd ed. F. L. Cross and E. A. Livingstone, Oxford U.P., 1997, p 600.) This relationship between faith, forgiveness and fasting is worth exploring. Believers down the ages have always known that by showing their gratitude to God, thankfulness is actually reinforced and extended. Our Lent response to the graciousness of God, in some form of self-denial, is both an expression of our faith and also encourages us to pursue our walk with God more deeply. Thankfulness is one of the wellsprings of religion – one of the ways in which our inner eye becomes more focused on the glory of God in apparently mundane routines.

The First Sunday of Lent

Deuteronomy 26:1–11; Psalm 91:1–2,9–16; Romans 10:8b-13;
Luke 4:1–13

Christian discipleship means following Jesus into an encounter with evil, sometimes personalized in scripture as an autonomous devil. In today's readings this is explored at a number of levels. The concern in Deuteronomy for the care of outsiders is a reminder of how often the stranger is demonized to carry deep fears and prejudices. Israelite faith will incorporate 'the aliens who reside among you' within the community.

From a rather different perspective Jesus is shown to be the fulfilment of the history of Israel, having a cosmic role in relation to evil. His followers are to recognize that even the roots of tragedy are within the very purpose of God as we experience it. The biblical tradition deals with this psychological reality in a number of ways; but contemporary insight supports the notion that suffering is neither a fate to be borne passively nor the ultimate enemy, but a process of growth to which all are summoned.

The passage from Deuteronomy, describing a harvest pilgrimage, remembers the exodus from Egypt as the formative event that had called a people into being. 'A wandering Aramaean . . .' stood at the centre of Israel's confession of faith from the beginning, and this invites us to trace our faith back to the experience of being foreigners, in the desert. It is a creed which incorporates the important insight, picked up in Luke's Gospel, that the wilderness is the place, both of testing, and of creative beginnings. In our thankfulness for nourishment and shelter, we are to remember not to externalize evil. Everything is grounded in God's love. God does not pull up evil by the roots, plead as we may, because the roots guarantee our freedom as we make our own desert journey.

In Paul's letters Jesus is often referred to as 'Lord', probably in answer to the many gods of the pagan religions. In this passage from Romans God's powers and reign are exercised through Christ as God's representative and things traditionally said about God may quite properly be said about Christ. In Paul's thinking the focus is on Jesus' stewardship of a ministry and mission delegated to him and shown in his life and death. The confession 'Jesus is Lord' is an individual commitment, and it is a lordship exercised over the Church corporately as well. Christian discipleship is always lived 'in the Lord' and, in New Testament terms, shares in the same cosmic conflict over which Jesus' ultimate and universal lordship is assured.

The Gospel reading sets Jesus' earthly ministry in that cosmic context. Luke saw the whole life of Jesus as one of temptation, which comes to a head in the passion. In the Bible this is the 'testing' of the true Son of God for his fidelity. The agent may be either God (as in the wilderness wanderings) or Satan (as in the story of Job). The immediate background for Luke's account is the wilderness temptations of Israel: Jesus succeeds where Israel fails (particularly in the supreme temptation of testing God) and so fulfils Israel's history.

It is on this larger canvas that Christian discipleship is to be understood. The call to 'embody Jesus' comes to the Church in barren and

---

Text

In Luke's version of the temptations Jesus has 'the power of the Spirit' (verse 14) and therefore no need of the angels with which both Mark and Matthew end their stories – on the model of Elijah in 1 Kings 19:4ff. Apart from Luke's 'he ate nothing' as against the more religious 'fasted', the most obvious difference between Matthew and Luke is in the different order of the temptations. Matthew follows Israel's temptations in the wilderness (according to Exodus chapters 16, 17 and 32), whereas Luke makes the temple temptation the climax of his story. Most commentators point out Luke's strong feelings towards Jerusalem and the temple as the place both of Jewish piety and of final sacrifice. Others suggest that the final temptation is linked in the tradition with 'you shall not put the Lord your God to the test' (4:12) which served Luke's purpose more decisively with its final word linking back neatly to the opening '. . . where for forty days he was tempted by the devil'. Both explanations are plausible.

The revisiting of 'evil' has been one of the tasks of twentieth-century philosophy and theology. Hopes of social progress through the spread of humanitarianism now seem rather naive: there are 'wild things' within – facing them is part of taming them.

---

wilderness places; but the ultimate harvest is cosmic and universal. It offers a vision which beckons us towards a more humane world as we endeavour to live the struggle with sin and evil in ourselves and our communities. We are not 'like God, knowing good and evil' in any absolute or final sense.

Psalm 9 is a favourite for Christian worship – notably for the late evening service of Compline. Very early in its history the text was assigned to different voices – pointing to its liturgical use in the Second Temple period from the fourth century BCE. (The Targums, interpretative renderings of the Hebrew Bible in Aramaic, date from the Persian administration and give us a good idea of how the Psalter was used.) Modern individualism, which assumes that worship is a private affair between the individual and God, is very alien to Israel's covenant faith according to which the individual is always related to God as a member of a community. To be a solitary individual, having 'no heritage of Yahweh' (1 Samuel 26.19), was a great calamity. The individual always praises God, as in this Psalm, with the worshipping community.

The Second Sunday of Lent

Genesis 15; Psalm 27; Philippians 3:17–4.1; Luke 13:31–35 *or* Luke 9:28–36

Today's exploration of discipleship is all about going beyond the vision, beyond the known and the understood. Two Gospel passages share a common concern with Jesus' prophetic status. Both allude to his impending rejection and understand this as being within the divine purpose. Similarly Paul writing to the Philippians seems determined to counter any euphoric and triumphalist teaching by stressing the suffering he shares with Christ. In our passage he encourages his fellow-Christians to follow this example.

The key factor in all this is that prayer lies at the heart of discipleship and may well represent the turning point towards suffering. Abram is viewed as the model for faith in the sense of responding trustingly to what God offers. The Old Testament passage reaffirms two strands in God's promise to him: the first is that Abram will be the father of countless descendants, and the second is the gift of a holy land. But a brief comment by the narrator holds the key. Abram trusts God, and it is this attitude of prayerful commitment, utter reliance going far beyond intellectual assent, which is the proper basis for facing whatever is to come. It is possible, perhaps necessary, to trust God in this way and yet live with very real uncertainties about the future. Such doubts are not the opposite of faith, but evidence of it. The final verse of Psalm 27 exhorts the disciple who prays and receives no answer to pray again and wait again in trust on the Holy One.

The theme of perseverance in the face of opposition continues as we move into the New Testament. Paul's relationship with the Philippians seems to have been a warm one. He wants to counter their spiritual enthusiasm with some earthy realism, hence the allusion to athletics to stress that the goal and transformation of Christians lies in the future. If there were Roman citizens in the congregation, the message would remind them that their citizenship of heaven takes precedence and will only be fulfilled with the return of the Lord Jesus.

The impression of a divinely destined itinerary, yet one that embraces earthly suffering, is reinforced in the passage from Luke 13.

Nothing will stop Jesus' prophetic ministry short of its appointed end. If he is to die, it will not be at Herod's hands but within God's purpose. His journey, the pattern for Christian discipleship, also has its goal in the future. The story of the transfiguration from Luke 9 provides another standpoint for understanding the coming rejection. The importance of Moses and Elijah underlines the focus on Jerusalem as the place both of suffering and of glory. Jesus, like them, is a supernatural figure and is fulfilling his divine destiny. Uniquely, the disciples are united with him in the cloud where they too have their call reaffirmed. They are the nucleus of the elect and are to receive his words as the words of God. In face of his divinely certified suffering, Jesus is nevertheless momentarily shown to be what he will eventually become. The whole scene is set in the context of a time of prayer with a theme of faithful trust in God's purpose. Uncertainty about how this will be fulfilled is no bar to discipleship, and the inner three are summoned from the mountain down to the plain and onwards to the further goal.

Text

It is usually reckoned that Luke has rewritten Mark's account of the transfiguration. Not all the changes are particularly instructive, but some are worth pursuing. For instance Luke omits the use of the word 'metamorphosis' from Mark, possibly to avoid association with pagan stories of this kind. Characteristically he pictures Jesus at prayer. He also draws much more strongly on the Old Testament tradition of divine appearances. The 'high mountain' becomes 'the mountain' of revelation, recalling Moses at Sinai and Elijah at Horeb. As the skin of Moses' face shone (Exodus 34:29) so the 'form of [Jesus'] face became altered'. Moses' exodus and Elijah's assumption may be in the evangelist's mind as he envisages Jesus' destiny which will take him to death and glory: they 'were speaking of his departure, which he was about to accomplish at Jerusalem' (9:31). Luke is less hard on Peter than Mark – in anticipation, perhaps, of the Gethsemane story where Peter and his companions are again overcome with sleep.

The Third Sunday of Lent

Isaiah 55:1–9; Psalm 63:1–8; 1 Corinthians 10:1–13; Luke 13:1–9

The disciple is summoned to a life-change – otherwise known as 'repentance'. We are inclined to see this as an onerous demand, but today's readings – without underestimating the difficulty – emphasize the gracious invitation which the Church's penitential season represents. The word-pictures range from rich banquets to wells of fresh water. These are contrasted with the sins and consequent disasters which deny access to these gifts.

The tone is set in the hymn from Isaiah which celebrates Israel's approaching restoration in terms very similar to Wisdom's invitation of Proverbs 9:1–6. The summons to a party includes the promise of pardon for all and a reminder that God who gives the pardon – and the party – may be found near at hand. The Psalm reiterates the theme of thirsting for God – a God who supplies our needs abundantly and whose grace is proffered to us as a free gift. The blessings of the past are renewed and set in a wider context. Israel's physical restoration is related to the restoration of her inner life – and this in turn is in response to a God who is central to the life of the whole world.

The New Testament reading remains with water and nourishment. Here it is the Christian rites of baptism and Eucharist which, in Paul's view, are being idolized by the Corinthians – some of whom feel secure, complacent because they have these sacraments. Like the Israelites before them (who were lured into destruction) so the idolatry of the Corinthians will offer no guarantees against harm. The Christian life is lived by faith only.

The strange story of the barren fig tree continues the thought of impending destruction – and is at the same time the basis for a summons to a change of life. It picks up the images of thirst and nourishment in the gardener's appeal for a year's stay of execution for the tree, reminding us, perhaps, that the life of faith needs time and will not necessarily comply with our impatience. The rich manure of experience, sin and misadventure needs to be dug in, and watered with the tears of penitence, before it will yield its fruits. But this is not simply an exhortation for individuals to repent of sin. It is also a prophetic warning that Israel as a nation is courting a disaster from which even religious people will not be exempt. Jesus' ministry offers the way forward for a whole society: our salvation is given to us corporately, inextricably bound up with changes in our common life. The party invitation is for everyone, and the people of God are summoned to make life-change sustainable at national and global levels.

Our present-day distinction between spiritual and physical makes the message of Second Isaiah (that is, Isaiah chapters 40–55) in this passage problematic. The prophet is not saying 'do not set your heart on earthly things . . . and strive for what is spiritual', but something much more like 'life in all its fullness is waiting for your return . . . . God is liberating you from Babylon **and** blessing you when you get home.' He is making a permanent covenant with his people, and the

---

Text

The outline of the parable of the fig tree seems to have reached Luke by way of the tradition, but he adds his own spin. As it stands in Mark, Jesus appears irrational in expecting fruit out of season. Luke recognizes that the force of the story is in its symbolism of the Jewish people, who do not bear fruit and are threatened by destruction. Luke seems to combine the fig tree incident with the parable of the man who planted a vineyard (Mark 12:1). To be saved one must repent and bear fruit. The parable is such an odd one. It either repels or intrigues. I have followed C. F. Evans (*St Luke*, SCM, 1990) in resisting the interpretation that '*if you do not repent [of sin in general] you will be condemned by God*'. There is a specific context: the destruction of the Jerusalem temple in 70 CE and the subsequent crushing of the Jewish nation seem to be in the evangelist's mind. The nation is being called to repentance; for Luke Jesus' lifetime gave that opportunity. But the tragedy has already unfolded.

For us, in the twenty-first century, terrible tragedy has also unfolded: the wars and massacres of our lifetime come from a propensity for cruelty combined with technology. The means for genocide have been fully developed. Only by addressing the destructive side of human psychology – corporately – can further disasters be averted.

promise to David is to be transferred to Israel. The passage set for today includes the first part of the final epilogue to this collection. The summons is to approach God and to turn towards him. God's designs are greater than we think them to be. All things are possible. As at the beginning of the collection, in Isaiah 40, God is praised as Creator and Lord of history, so here the people are to be encouraged by the great height of his 'thoughts' and 'ways'.

The Fourth Sunday of Lent

Joshua 5:9–12; Psalm 32; 2 Corinthians 5:16–21;
Luke 15:1–3,11b-32

Coming home to a party in the land of promise and to the embrace of a loving father signals an uplifting and joyful experience. Today brings a different perspective to the Lenten encounter with evil and to the call to repentance. We are to turn round and see that we have crossed the river and that God has already surrounded us with loving acceptance. The image of a nourishing banquet, prepared for all, permeates the readings.

The passage from Joshua describes the keeping of Passover at Gilgal. The story follows on from the circumcision of a whole new generation of Israelites, a sign of their covenant with the God who has 'rolled away . . . the disgrace of Egypt' and who now feeds them with the produce of the land of Canaan. God's people are not slaves but free agents. No longer must they eat manna in the wilderness; that debt is paid and they have come home to the land of promise. The Psalm likewise celebrates the joy of forgiveness – and of healing, commonly linked with it. The frail and wasted body will be sustained by nourishment and give evidence of God's favour.

In Jewish tradition neither sickness nor death was part of God's plan for humanity. This gets Paul into a fix when he comes to proclaim the gospel of Christ – since it is precisely the *death* of Jesus which he understands as effecting salvation. God's forgiveness reaches out to his creatures, but in their turn they have to renounce sin. Paul continues this appeal, reminding the Corinthians that assenting to the 'theory' is not sufficient – they should also conform to Christ in their behaviour. It will be their own freely-made decision which will reconcile them with God.

The story of the two brothers and their father is told, in the context of a meal, to two very separate groups of people. The 'tax-collectors and sinners' are marginalized by Jewish society and the 'scribes and Pharisees' believe themselves to *be* Jewish society. In this parable Jesus invites both groups to the banquet. The outcasts are to hear God's unconditional welcome and forgiveness; the 'righteous' may discover that, like the elder brother, they are in danger of excluding themselves from a continuous party. The freedom to refuse

God's invitation to discipleship remains integral to the gift that is on offer. Human response and co-operation are won by love always – by coercion never. It is the younger son who, of his own volition, decides no longer to eat the filth to which his choices have led him, but to return and eat at his father's table.

Background

The Passover – the great festival in Judaism of remembering the past – has become in recent years more poignant yet: the time to remember family members separated by death and distance and twentieth-century genocide. Since earliest times the Jewish Passover had an attraction for Christians, because it was the occasion for Jesus' Last Supper. So widely prevalent was the joint feasting of Christians with Jews on the Passover that in 341 the Council of Antioch (Canon 1) passed legislation prohibiting Christians from doing so (cited by Louis Feldman, *Jew and Gentile in the Ancient World*, Princeton U.P., 1993, p 376).

Mothering Sunday

Exodus 2:1–10 *or* 1 Samuel 1:20–28; Psalm 34:11–20 *or* Psalm 127:1–4; 2 Corinthians 1:3–7 *or* Colossians 3:12–17; Luke 2:33–35 *or* John 19:25–27

Mothering Sunday services tend to be bright and breezy, with much participation by children who say and do nice things for their mums and grandmas, and the service usually develops the theme of family life in some aspect. It can all be rather cosy and un-realistic – because mothers the world over know the true story. Motherhood is no bed of roses. How realistic the Bible is! Here we meet motherhood in the raw. The two Gospel passages are alter-natives, but they complement each other, for in Luke 2 Simeon foresees the 'sword' which John 19 then describes. When Mary heard Simeon's prophecy, she must have been horrified. But never in her worst nightmares can she have imagined that, some thirty-three years later, she would stand beside a Roman cross and watch her dear Son gasp his life away in agony.

John describes the scene so sparingly. It must have cost Mary every ounce of strength in her body not to hurl herself against the Roman guard, shouting Jesus' innocence and crying for his release. How could they sit there, calmly tearing up his clothes and casting lots for them! But she knew that this was his 'hour', the moment he had foreseen and had not sought to avoid. It would be disloyalty to him to protest and resist – unjust, vile, crushing though it was. So she just has to stand there, leaning on her sister and her two friends – three Marys together – and absorb the pain as the sword went through her soul. Even in his agony Jesus knows what she is going through, and lovingly connects her with the one disciple who will be able to explain a little of what his death means, and why it had to be.

Yes, motherhood can be agony. Moses' mother Jochebed (Exodus 2) had to choose between having her baby killed or trusting him to God in a wicker basket on the Nile. Samuel's mother Hannah (1 Samuel 1) simply knew that she had to give her son up: she would keep him for a while, but as soon as he could cope she would give him back to the God who had given him to her. So our readings present us with three mothers who gave their children away to God – under very different circumstances, but all with pain, and with joy.

The joy came through the pain, and after it. All three tell us that our children are not ours, but God's, that we have them on trust from him, that we cannot 'possess' them and make them what we want, but only love them, nurture them, and give them away. Only the God and Father of our Lord Jesus Christ can make such giving joyful – because he too has given away a Son. And because of that gift we may have hope for our children, whatever happens to them.

Mary knew in a unique way what Paul expresses in 2 Corinthians 1, as he writes of sharing the suffering of Christ, so that ultimately comfort may overflow from Christ to us, and through us to others also. Paul feels for his churches the same 'motherly' agony, the same longing to communicate all he has learned of Christ, the same frustration when they fail to respond, the same need for an unshakeable hope (2 Corinthians 1:7) founded on the sufferings of Christ for us.

The Fifth Sunday of Lent

Isaiah 43:16–21; Psalm 126; Philippians 3:4b–14; John 12:1–8

The Lenten exploration of discipleship brings us to the threshold of Holy Week. The readings of this season have led inexorably towards the presentation of Jesus' passion as a triumphant climax to his healing and prophetic ministry. This is reinforced in John's Gospel where he is entirely in control of all that happens to him both before (10:17) and during the trial ('you have no power over me', 19:11). The readings all focus on questions of identity. The little group of disciples, still on its way to Jerusalem, will be transformed into a community and empowered by Jesus' triumphant return to the Father. But first there is a dinner party. Here at Bethany, in his encounter both with Mary and with Judas Iscariot, the matter of Jesus's identity comes to the fore as he is anointed king – a sign for his followers that God turns the world of appearances entirely upside down.

The reading from Isaiah 43 gives a similar sense of being on the brink of great salvific events. Again, the people formed to declare God's praise stand on the threshold of a new identity. It is a work of God which fulfils a vision that can only be barely glimpsed. It signals a change of fortune – the greening of the desert place. The Psalm intimates that the going out and returning home 'carrying sheaves' will nourish and sustain God's people. The Philippian Church, in the New Testament, is similarly summoned to embrace a new calling. Paul is warning them to beware of complacency and of putting confidence in religious institutions. He exhorts them to accept an identity as resurrection people, imitating him: 'Forgetting what lies behind and straining forward to what lies ahead, I press on toward the goal for the prize of the heavenly call of God in Christ Jesus.'

In John's Gospel the crucifixion is set in the context of Passover celebrations. This gives Jesus' death a sacrificial significance. There is a sense of 'straining forward' towards the deliverance of God's people. Jesus will be 'enthroned' on the cross, so Mary's anointing is both a recognition of his royal dignity and an anticipation of his burial. Her own identity is not developed beyond this apparently unconscious prophetic act. By contrast, Judas is portrayed posturing behind a mask of piety. He knows the law – but in his own

66

dishonesty is resisting any true claim upon his life. Jesus' ministry as prophet and healer is reviewed and confirmed, and his new royal and priestly identity carries him forward 'toward the goal'.

Background

Reflected in ancient customs from around the world is the belief that the time of sowing was a time of mourning. In ancient Egypt, for instance, sowing was accompanied by funeral hymns to Osiris. It underlies the New Testament parable of the grain of wheat (John 12:24; Corinthians 15:36). In Psalm 126 the metaphor relates to present calamities in which the author sees the mysterious power of God creating new life. Suffering and death are part of God's work of redemption, but the autumn Feast of Ingathering, at which the Israelites recited this Psalm, was not purely an annual celebration of the natural cycle, but a reminder also of God's gracious activity throughout history.

Palm Sunday

Isaiah 50:4–9a; Psalm 31:9–16; Philippians 2:5–11;
Luke 22:14–23,56 *or* Luke 23:1–49

A world turned upside down and a reversal of values have been features of the Lenten exploration of discipleship. The requirement of the followers of Jesus is that they live in counter-culture to their own society including, almost certainly, their religious institutions. On Palm Sunday the readings dramatize this topsy-turvy theme without flinching from the tragedy which it implies. For in Luke's Gospel Jesus is a tragic figure, and we have the opportunity to examine this today through three different accounts.

The first is the acclamation of Jesus by his disciples before he enters the city of Jerusalem. The Pharisees appear, for the last time in Luke's Gospel, as their opponents. Even the stones of Jerusalem can recognize Jesus' royal status. It is quite simply rejected by the Jewish leaders. The second scene is Luke's account of the Last Supper, and here the emphasis is on the Messianic Banquet, where the destitute would enjoy whatever they lacked in this world. In an unjust society Jesus inaugurates a foretaste of paradise – where Christians are renewed as one body through participation in one loaf (1 Corinthians 10). He manages to emphasize both a physical satisfaction which is a present experience and also a perfect satisfaction in the next life. The echoes of Mary's Magnificat, in which the familiar world is turned upside down, ring through clearly. Thirdly, the passion narrative from Luke expresses the rejection of God's chosen one by God's people, and reiterates the humiliation endured by Jesus, the one who should have been most honoured. It's a topsy-turvy world – and Luke is uniquely able to reinforce the evil of the moment because he will take a second volume to show how the Holy Spirit empowers the missionary work of the Church and vindicates the tragedy.

Confidence that God will reverse his fortunes – and the fortunes of Israel – is expressed by the servant in the Old Testament reading from Isaiah. The famous passage from Philippians describes Jesus in similar terms as a humble slave, obedient to the point of death, who is nevertheless exalted to the glory of God the Father. The power struggle between Paul and his Jewish Christian opponents, described

68

in this letter, seems to have focused on the necessity for suffering – his own and that of Christ – in contrast to the complacency encouraged by his rivals. He goes on from this passage to spell out the implications for discipleship in terms of standing against the prevailing values: 'That you may be . . . children of God without blemish in the midst of a crooked and perverse generation.'

The 'hymn' of Philippians 2 has been the focus of much speculation as one of the most important Christological passages in the New Testament. Issues such as its authorship and provenance, its independence of the rest of the letter and the extent to which it reflects Wisdom speculation have all been hotly debated. Usually it is cited as an example of the rapid development of ideas of incarnation and the 'divinity' and pre-existence of Jesus. Paul's stress, however, is on the suffering and death of Jesus. His enthronement in heaven is to be seen here – as in the Letter to the Hebrews – as the consequence of a life of willing obedience. Like many other New Testament authors, Paul is indebted to Psalm 110. '*The Lord says to my Lord, "Sit at my right hand until I make your enemies your footstool."*' (Psalm 110:1)

Text

Luke's passion narrative expands the Roman side of Mark's story. His whole account of the trial is designed to blame the Jewish leadership and exonerate Pilate and the Romans. The usual explanation has been that Luke is aiming to get increased toleration for Christian beliefs and practices, but it is also probable that his community included a number of Romans serving the empire. If this is so, his aim is also to reassure them that faith in Jesus Christ and allegiance to Rome are not mutually exclusive. The freedom with which Luke has told his story is encouraging for all who want to make sense of the Christian vision in terms of their own time.

The Monday of Holy Week

Isaiah 42:1–9; Psalm 36:5–11; Hebrews 9:11–15; John 12:1–11

People with power like to hang on to it. We are all in danger of measuring our status in terms of the rewards that we receive. The coronation service for a British monarch rightly emphasizes the responsibility of those with power to give service rather than receive it. When we proclaim Jesus as a 'king', all sorts of questions concerned with the use and abuse of such power immediately surface. It is a debate which lies at the heart of the Holy Week quest for Jesus' true identity. What we make of him – this week of all weeks – determines what we make of God.

Today the mood shifts noticeably from the innocent martyrdom of Luke's tragedy to the more regal preliminaries for 'enthronement' in John's Gospel. In full knowledge of a plot, Jesus returns to Bethany and is anointed by Mary 'six days before Passover'. This connection with Passover flags up the approaching sacrifice, while Jesus himself remains in control of all that happens. The threat to Lazarus' life is a reminder of the implications for faithful discipleship. We are offered an overarching theme for the week: the anointing of Jesus as king already reinterprets tragedy – his burial and ours – in the light of future exaltation.

There can have been no more poignant tragedy for first-century Jewish Christians than the destruction of the Jerusalem Temple in 70CE. The author of the Letter to the Hebrews points to Jesus' enthronement as a sign that all sacrifice is now redundant. He reigns, not on the cross as in the Gospel, but in heaven – in the presence of God, a state promised to the faithful, and this assures them of their salvation. Hebrews challenges all our attempts to localize God in our own religious institutions. Here the death and exaltation of Jesus is the replacement for Israel's previous means of access to God. His present enthronement in heaven has been achieved by faithful obedience. A death willingly accepted in obedience to the will of God is what makes his the superior sacrifice. The superior sinlessness of Jesus lies in his life-long obedience to God which culminates in the cross. Hebrews is preoccupied with Jesus' present enthronement in heaven – achieved by faithful obedience. The gospel of human liberation means that everything else must serve that cause.

The Old Testament reading identifies the servant with Israel ('my chosen') who will, with all patience, bring God's teaching and justice to the nations. The prophecies of Second Isaiah (that is, Isaiah chapters 40–55) affirm that Israel – sometimes personified as prophet or king – will be exalted through suffering. When, in the Gospel, Mary anoints Jesus for his burial, it is the same kingdom of justice and freedom which is being announced. Jesus' royal identity, like that of the people of God, is the gift of God and bears fruit in service and in suffering.

Interpretation

The four Servant Songs from the 'Babylonian Chapters' of the book of Isaiah are all set during Holy Week: on Monday, Tuesday, Wednesday and Friday. The poems, which may originally have described the imprisoned king or the prophet himself, were taken messianically by many Jews in the period following the exile. They were popular for that reason with the first Christians, who saw in them a foretelling of Jesus as suffering Messiah. Considerably worked over and reinterpreted during the exile, they lend themselves to multiple interpretation and are often seen as telling the story of the whole people of God collectively. They offer rich fare for meditation during this week as Christians seek to follow Jesus along the way of the cross.

The Tuesday of Holy Week

Isaiah 49:1–7; Psalm 71:1–14; 1 Corinthians 1:18–31;
John 12:20–36

Ethnic conflicts indicate, as we know from history, that religion has its dark side. Genuine religion unites; distorted religion divides. The Holy Week quest for Jesus' true identity is continued in an exploration of light and darkness – a theme which will be pursued through the days leading up to his death. John's Gospel shows us the conflict in language normally reserved for apocalyptic 'end-time' events: it is as Son of Man that Jesus forms the connecting link between the earthly and heavenly spheres. His lifting up to die is also his exaltation in glory, enabling everyone (including Gentile Greeks) to be drawn to God. Meanwhile he remains hidden and unrecognized. This Gospel always shows Jesus as in command of the situation: characteristically the struggle with God over his destiny is resolved by divine affirmation almost before it is uttered.

Jesus' identity as Son of Man, explored in terms of light and darkness, has its mysterious side. Now you see him; now you don't. Jesus' future glory is visible to the eye of faith, but faith sees it most fully in darkness and suffering. Thus it has ever been. The servant of the Lord is identified in Isaiah's prophecies with faithful Israel, and over the years has been applied to chosen individuals, so that the people of God may fulfil their destiny as 'light for the nations'.

Paul, in the First Letter to the Corinthians, also sees the heart of the gospel in the cross of Jesus. Like John he announces it as a mystery 'foolishness to those who are perishing'. The word 'wisdom' seems to have been misunderstood in Corinth. Paul allows it in 2:5, but prefers God's 'power' for the present. For Paul the 'wisdom of God' is in direct conflict with the 'wisdom of the world' and is demonstrated above all in the folly of the cross. This is nothing to do with abstract or speculative thought, but more to do with recognizing God's authority and living in relationship with him. Closely associated with the work of God in creation, 'wisdom' in the Old Testament is the fulfilment of 'sensual' knowledge and exemplifies the biblical understanding of this relationship at its best. We fail to apprehend God in creation only because of our own self-regarding wisdom. Tempting the Lord – the sin of the desert (Numbers

14:11,22) – implies a refusal to take God on trust and to worship our own image instead. Similarly, in the New Testament, the 'secret of the kingdom' is grasped by those on the edges – the Gentiles, the women, the socially or religiously marginalized – rather than by the disciples.

So, according to Paul, God's glory and wisdom remain hidden because human beings prefer to worship their own image. Jesus' mysterious identity and the meaning of his death elude definition. It is in his death that he returns to the Father. With apparent forethought and intention John refers to it in terms of the final victory at the end of time. It is left to his followers to realize the fullness of that victory. But first, recognizing that they walk in light, not darkness, they are to seek out the hidden wisdom – a means of new and relational experience for all God's people.

Interpretation

Addressing the Gentiles in this second Servant Song, the servant explains his commission, his despondency and the ultimate extension of the commission to include the Gentiles. The main difficulty in the interpretation of the passage is that the servant of verse 3, Israel, is in verse 5 given a mission to Israel. But almost certainly the 'Israel' in verse 3 is an early gloss, giving a collective interpretation to the servant for the first time. The disgrace of suffering is more often associated with individual humiliation. We are less familiar with this kind of shame, whereas in ancient Israel it seems to have been inseparably linked to sickness and grief (witness the books of Lamentations and Job).

The Wednesday of Holy Week

Isaiah 50:4–9a; Psalm 70; Hebrews 12:1–3; John 13:21–32

An exploration of Jesus' identity in terms of being both Son of Man and anointed King is now pursued in terms of Jesus as Prophet. For Luke's Gospel, this was the overarching theme: Jesus the prophet destined to fulfil all prophecy. In John's Gospel it also has its place. Jesus reveals the Father, and those who witness the revelation choose either true or false discipleship. Again Jesus is presented as being in control of the situation: as Lord of good and evil and of light and darkness. Today, with the prediction of his betrayal by Judas, the darkness of the night begins to close in ominously.

The reading from Isaiah describes the prophet pursuing his calling to 'sustain the weary with a word', while at the same time facing ridicule and judgment in a court of law. Confronting the adversary and the false friend in open trial adds a poignancy to the background to the Last Supper. God leads the servant safely through the darkness of rejection; by contrast, those who walk by their own lights will

---

Text

In the Synoptic Gospels the plot to betray Jesus to the Jewish authorities happens on the Wednesday. In John, Jesus has come to Jerusalem on a number of occasions and many of the synoptic Holy Week events have been spread over these visits. A Sanhedrin session, led by Caiaphas, has taken place more than a week before Passover. There is a looming sense that Jesus is attracting too many people and that the temple is under threat from the Romans. John's chronology is different from the other three Gospels partly in order to make closer links between Jesus' death and the Passover. Here at the Last Supper with his disciples the overall atmosphere is one of love, unity and leave-taking. There are no eucharistic words (these things have been dealt with in chapter 6) but extended farewell discourses will heighten the anticipation of tragedy and glory.

---

perish in the night. This may be extended to God's chosen people; both Israel and the Church are called to walk in the light and to project it into the darkness.

The author of Hebrews presents Jesus as a pioneer whose pilgrimage has brought him to the 'promised land' of heaven where he is exalted to the right hand of God. He has gained access to the only sacred space worth having – so his friends should not hanker after alternatives such as the Jerusalem Temple. The passage is primarily an exhortation to perseverance, distinguishing between faithful precursors of faith (including Jesus) and the faithlessness of the wilderness wanderings. The exalted Christ is not a distant figure. His return is anticipated very soon.

John is preoccupied with Judas' treachery – and his fascination with the theme of loyalty and disloyalty suggests that he writes for a prophetic community threatened by outside pressures. Today it is a bitter betrayal of companionship which comes to the fore, but true friendship will also find its place in the story.

Maundy Thursday

Exodus 12:1-4, 11-14 *or* 1–14; Psalm 116:1-2,12–19;
1 Corinthians 11:23–26; John 13:1–17,31b-35

Our Holy Week exploration of who Jesus truly is comes to the heart of the matter with his presentation of himself as 'servant' and as 'teacher'. John's Gospel sets the killing of Jesus at the same time as the killing of sacrificial lambs for Passover, so this last meal with his friends is not the occasion for the institution of the Eucharist in this Gospel. Instead, an account of the foot-washing is included and it is Jesus' self-sacrificing humility which is shown to us as an expression of his love for his friends. All the disciples save one are clean, and therefore fitted for Christ's service through their faith and loyalty. But even they who are already bathed must allow their feet to be washed. Forgiveness is the hallmark of the service which Jesus offers. True friendship and loyal discipleship are renewed by example.

The Exodus event was so crucial to the religion of Israel that it was used to inaugurate a new calendar and was commemorated with an annual festival. By the gracious action of God an enslaved people was set free and led through the wilderness to the promised land. This deliverance is made present whenever the Passover is sacrificed and celebrated. The story is rehearsed in the present tense. Each generation makes it their own and it has upheld the Jewish people in every major crisis from that day to this.

Paul regarded Jesus as the new Christian Passover. For Jews, the Passover was and is the sacrifice and festival of God's deliverance, and for him Jesus has effected something similar. This is represented in the Last Supper which became the Christian memorial supper. Paul reinforces the connection between the supper and the death of Christ – for him the heart of the gospel. When Christians hold a common meal they recall aloud the event on which their existence is based. This recalling originally resembled the narration of the exodus from Egypt. The repetition is to continue until Jesus returns; and there can be little doubt that Paul expected this in his lifetime. The timescale gives an urgency and an immediacy to the narrative.

The quest for Jesus' true identity has almost reached its end. In John's Gospel the trial before Pilate brings it to a climax – but this supper scene lays a vital foundation: it is Jesus the servant and teacher who determines the character of the kingdom which he will inaugurate with his death. Without the example of self-giving love or the treachery of a friend, our own questions may well remain rather abstract. As it is, our search for God is to be earthed in human community.

Theology

The experience of exile, prison or homesickness is often a spur to remembrance. To be uprooted is to begin a search for the meaning of the past – an attempt to put it all together. The life of faith is not a 'belief-system' and prayer is one of the most significant ways of stepping beyond ourselves, so that our awareness is extended to incorporate the universe – including our own past – and to embrace suffering. Nelson Mandela comes to mind – and his statement from the dock in 1962, facing an almost certain death sentence: 'I have cherished the ideal of a democratic and free society in which persons live together in harmony and with equal opportunities. It is an ideal which I hope to live for and to achieve. But, if needs be, it is an ideal for which I am prepared to die.'

Good Friday

Isaiah 52:13–53:12; Psalm 22; Hebrews 10:16–25 *or*
Hebrews 4:14–16; 5:7–9; John 18:1–19,42

On Good Friday the great themes of the penitential season all come together: hypocrisy is exposed, Jesus' identity is judged, the Roman governor is converted. The overwhelming message of the readings is that all who are oppressed, but who retain a sense that God is with them, will come to recognize how little jurisdiction any worldly authority really has. There is an exploration of what it means to move in and out of a sense of God's presence.

The servant – originally perhaps the imprisoned king or victimized prophet – is also to be understood as the suffering and exiled people of God. In many ways this 'Song of the Servant' is a Passion narrative with which it is easier to identify than the triumphant portrait of Jesus in John's Gospel. Constantly worked over, through hundreds of years, it is able to interpret both personal and national events with power and poignancy. The psalmist, similarly, is a person of influence and authority in an unexpected situation of helplessness. Psalm 22 is, after all, ascribed to King David! There is raw emotion in the language; the Psalmist 'roars' (verse 1) like a lion in his anger and bewilderment, and there is a grandiose dimension in the powerful animals and the call to all the nations. The central issue is trust in God. The psalmist feels utterly betrayed, and there is a bitter contrast between the religious language of God's presence and the powerful experience of God's distance in his time of need: 'My God! My God, why . . . ?'

The movement from distance to presence – and endurance for the task – is a dominant motif in Hebrews. An appeal to God's faithfulness is the basis to a call for similar faithfulness on the part of the Christian group which is being addressed. The attainment of God's purposes always lies in the future; only Jesus has already entered his presence – but Christians are encouraged to follow him as they approach heaven themselves. The bar to access is guilt – and it is the author's conviction that this has been removed through the sacrifice of Christ. Jesus' suffering and humanity are the source of his effectiveness as 'priest' – but it is to his exaltation that Christians are to look for encouragement. The notion of perfection and sinlessness is best understood in the context of the Day of Atonement rituals, in which sacrifice was integral to the process. It is by his sacrifice that Jesus attains heaven, the true Holy of Holies. In death he is, by this analogy, both priest and victim. Primarily, however, he is God's unique and obedient son – in the traditional Jewish understanding of suffering as God's disciplining of his children. Hebrews concentrates on the effect rather than the cause of the crucifixion and so has no need to stress the injustice of the cross. Unlike today's Gospel Passion narrative, for this author sacrifice and exaltation are not fused but are two separate acts.

In John's Gospel the Jerusalem authorities have tried to seize or kill Jesus several times. In the face of this hostility he sets the sovereign tone early on: 'I lay down my life . . . I lay it down of my own accord' (10:17). It is those who come to arrest him who fall back to the ground, helpless. The trial scene is more a judgment of Pilate than of Jesus, and the burial is that of a king who has ruled from the cross. All in all it is a story seen with the eyes of faith. But, within it, there is a narrative of Pilate moving from incomprehension and fear to an extraordinary acknowledgement of Jesus' power and authority. Typical of John is the constant movement of the Roman governor in and out of his palace. There is indecision, the attempt to do the right thing, weakness and ignorance. One man's struggle with unbelief and his conscience (occasionally echoed in the behaviour of Peter the disciple) gives texture to the message that apparent distance from God's love may paradoxically be the place of conversion, the discovery of God's nearer presence.

Easter Eve

Job 14:1–14 *or* Lamentations 3:1–9,19–24; Psalm 31:1–4,15–16;
1 Peter 4:1–8; Matthew 27:57–66 *or* John 19:38–42

The mood of today's readings follows the events described in the Gospels. From Matthew's account there is finality, sadness, an affirmation of God's constancy but little assurance for the future. From John's account there is the grandeur of a royal burial, but it is somewhat anticlimactic after the enthronement and exaltation of the king on the cross. The story of Jesus' burial meets Christians in a place of confused anticipation, and the other readings echo both the hope and the bereavement.

Lamentations and Job date from the period of the exile. Job seems to be addressed to those in captivity, but Lamentations is aimed at those who remained amongst the ruins. The sufferings of Judah are described and attributed to the direct activity of God's judgment. So bitter was the anguish and so oppressive the burden that the author could not banish it from his thoughts. Only the realization that long-overdue penitence was now clearly evident enabled him to hold out any hope at all for the future. Both authors give magnificent expressions of faith in the covenant mercies of God and are able to look to the distant future with renewed optimism.

The First Letter of Peter portrays Jesus as the new Enoch who, in Jewish apocalyptic tradition, visited the underworld to seal the doom of all the evil powers associated with Satan. The main reason for the letter is to encourage an isolated Christian group in their discipleship, so this assurance of God's overall control is well suited to their situation. It finds an echo whenever people feel at the mercy of ruthless forces, and 'He descended into hell' survives today in the Apostles' Creed. What may have begun in 1 Peter as a way to emphasize Jesus' identification with the human lot was expanded to hold out the hope that all are within the scope of salvation. The letter itself is not so positive about universal salvation and warns readers against the temptation to avoid suffering by assimilating to alien ways.

All the Gospels attribute Jesus' burial to Joseph of Arimathea. Matthew's narrative particularly leaves us in no doubt that Jesus really died and was buried. It reminds readers of the suffering servant of Isaiah, and the setting of the guard alerts them to a possible but false explanation of the empty tomb. Matthew writes to convince us that Jesus was indeed the one promised by God in scripture. He seems to have known that his readers would be confronted with Jewish criticism of Jesus as a magician and deceiver; he tackles the sceptics head-on. John makes rather more of Joseph and Nicodemus, who in his Gospel believe 'secretly' until this moment. Now they come publicly – in the light – as all believers must. There has been a gradual conversion – a movement, like that of Pontius Pilate, towards discipleship. This may be an encouragement to other synagogue leaders to follow the same way. Like Pilate they seem to acknowledge Jesus as king, using the huge amounts of spices associated with royal burials and giving him a garden sepulchre like that associated with King David.

Jesus' burial, like all burials, faces us with our mortality. It makes us sad; but, as often, it is loss which brings us up short, and enables us to stop hedging our bets and to live fearlessly with our true choices. Joseph and Nicodemus offer a model of faith for the cautious and sceptical of every age.

Background

Joseph of Arimathea, the secret disciple, is one of the Bible's mysterious figures about whom we know very little. According to the apocryphal 'Gospel of Nicodemus' he played an important part in the foundation of the first Christian community at Lydda. There is a thirteenth-century legend that he came to England with the Holy Grail and built the first church in the country at Glastonbury. But as the Abbey at Glastonbury is also linked with King Arthur, St Dunstan and St Patrick, this story may be wishful thinking!

Easter Day

Acts 10:34–43 *or* Isaiah 65:17–25; Psalm 118:1–2,14–24;
1 Corinthians 15:19–26 *or* Acts 10:34–43; John 20:1–18 *or*
Luke 24:1–12

There are many choices to be made about the readings today; what does the preacher want the people to hear? How do we best celebrate this central feast of the Christian calendar? It is entirely appropriate that a kaleidoscope of themes should be present in the readings on this day, the most important in the Christian year, for the whole spectrum of believing is brought into the focus of our vision of Jesus, the crucified, now raised again from the dead. But that does not mean that the task is easy!

The reading from the penultimate chapter of the book of Isaiah belongs to the third section of that prophecy, and it deals with the hope, on the part of those who have returned from exile, that God will accomplish new things for Jerusalem. The picture painted is almost utopian, with no violence, no natural disasters and no family sadnesses; even the animals will cease to feed off one another.

The psalmist in Psalm 118 celebrates the king's entry into the temple at the autumn festival. He experiences a ritual humiliation, in order to know a triumphant glorification, and in doing so he embodies the life of his people. He feels the pain of rejection, but exults in the joy of restoration, like a stone at first rejected by the builders, but now made into the most significant in the building.

These themes of the new age and of glorious renewal naturally echo Christian joy at the resurrection of Jesus. His new life is the life of the new age which God inaugurates when he establishes his final kingdom; and where he reigns in resurrected glory, there is peace among the whole of creation. St Paul is expressing this connection when he speaks of a hope which extends beyond this world to the age to come. For him, as well as for all the earliest disciples, the resurrection of Jesus marked the start of the coming of the end, when God would return to vindicate his people and establish his kingdom on earth. St Peter's experience draws different implications from the story; his decision to baptize Gentiles expressed his sense of God's call to all people for inclusion in the divine purposes.

All this – and more – derives from these simple yet complex stories of a group of women – or one woman! – going to the tomb of Jesus on the third day after his crucifixion and finding his body no longer there. Our choice of Gospel to read will determine the flavour of the story we hear. St Luke tells of a group of women, three of whom he names, whose perplexity turns to recall of the words of Jesus and joyful spreading of the news. The focus then switches to Peter, who looks in and sees the linen cloths and returns home 'amazed'.

St John's is a more personal and 'romantic' version of the story. Peter's run becomes a race with the 'disciple whom Jesus loved', who outruns him; nevertheless it is Peter who enters the tomb first. It has been suggested that the disciple whom Jesus loved represents the 'ideal' disciple, whether an historical figure or not, whom St John portrays as close to Jesus in his trials, and the first to believe in his resurrection.

The focus then shifts to Mary Magdalene. All we are told of her in the New Testament is that she was at the tomb on the morning of the resurrection, ready to anoint the body of Jesus, and that, according to Luke 8:2, 'seven demons had gone out' from her. This tradition is repeated in the 'shorter ending' to Mark (at 16:9), with the additional information that it was Jesus who had cast them out. Her touching story has provided imagery for all who at first have not seen, but whose weeping has been turned to joy when they have been addressed by the risen Lord.

Text

Easter is a marvellous occasion for pointing out the differences in the details of the stories which the evangelists tell, for they each have different numbers of women going to the tomb on Easter morning. This is not something to be afraid of, nor should the preacher pretend that discrepancies between the four Gospels do not exist: they are testimony to the variety of responses which the conviction of the living presence of Jesus generates.

The Second Sunday of Easter

Acts 5:27–32; Psalm 118:14–29 *or* Psalm 150; Revelation 1:4–8;
John 20:19–31

There is a sense in which it is curious that there should be any 'Easter Sunday' and 'Sundays of Easter' at all, for every Sunday is the Festival of Easter. In the first place, celebration of the living presence of Jesus is not restricted to an annual festival, and, secondly, the Church from its earliest days celebrated every week the belief that Jesus was alive again after his death. That is why we have Sunday as the first day of the week in our calendar – even if our printed diaries give scant recognition of the fact! However, the same might be said against a weekly observance of Easter: why not a reminder of and thanksgiving for the resurrection of Jesus every day?

This is where Christian living and prayer come in. According to the Acts of the Apostles, the life of the earliest Church was characterized by boldness, confidence, praise and peace; and these are marks, both of Christian living and of Christian praying.

The Acts of the Apostles provides us with a defence of the early Christian community before the Roman authorities; these are no troublemakers, but loyal, devout members of society, who want to have the freedom to worship and to go about their business as believers in the risen Jesus. When this lifestyle conflicts with the demands of the authorities, then they are prepared to stand their ground and defend their position with boldness.

A different kind of boldness, or confidence, is what marks Psalm 118. Here the praying community expresses its confidence in the victory of God. One of the earliest strands of reflection on the significance of the resurrection of Jesus is his victory over the forces of evil; and that conviction forms the background to one of the first theories of the atonement.

Psalm 150 gives no particular reason for praising God; it just gets on with it. Lovers don't keep asking why they are loved; they rejoice in the knowledge that they are. Here all kinds of musical instruments are invoked to join in the praise of God; especially on this day, the Church of Jesus Christ wants 'everything that has breath' to join in the praises of him who raised Jesus from the dead, so that we too might be raised from suffering, from sin and from all that makes for death in human experience.

At the root of all this confidence and praise is the story of the presence of Jesus. According to John's resurrection story, one of the apostles, Thomas, had been absent when the risen Lord had shown himself to the disciples on the evening of the resurrection. This detail of the earlier story makes possible the statement which applies to all of us who have believed in Jesus since those earliest days, 'Blessed are those who have not seen and yet believe!' The gift of the peace of Christ is the constant factor between those days and our own; to know him is to love him, and to love him is to know ourselves already loved by him; and if by him, then by God, his Father and ours.

To these stories are added the opening story from the Book of Revelation concerning John's call to write the vision which he saw. For the writer of this amazing book the impetus to writing was provided by the same Spirit who raised Jesus from the dead and who inspires the Christian life of prayer and confidence.

Interpretation

Reference has been made above to 'atonement', the network of convictions about how people are reconciled, or 'made one', with God in the light of the reality of suffering and wrongdoing. How is the idea of victory over the forces of evil to be understood, both in a day which is separated from the resurrection by two millennia and by ways of thinking which reject the influence of spirits as the inspiration of human behaviour?

The Third Sunday of Easter

Acts 9:1–6 *or* 1–20; Psalm 30; Revelation 5:11–14; John 21:1–19

Whatever else the resurrection is about, it certainly has to do with new beginnings. Today's readings speak of two such.

The call of St Paul has become a classic narrative of our culture. A 'Damascus Road' experience is a symbol of conversion, of repentance, of a change of mind. The details of the story are etched in our memories. We have all stood by as Paul is blinded; we have looked with Paul on the inside of our eyelids and seen the darkness; we have felt the hesitation of Ananias; we have been moved at this one disciple's obedience; we have wept with joy at this turning to God on the part of a former persecutor, who is to become such a formidable protagonist for the gospel; and we have also shuddered at the warning, 'I myself will show him how much he must suffer for the sake of my name.'

This is a story of what can happen when one person is confronted by the living Christ; the language of newness is the only language possible. But at the centre of that newness remains the image of crucifixion, for this is how the newness is brought about: the freshness of resurrection life is purchased at the cost of sacrificial love. So there is a connection between the self-disclosure of Jesus as 'the one whom you are persecuting' and his promise to Ananias: 'I myself will show him how much he must suffer for the sake of my name.' The servant will not be above his Master. These are the grounds for praise at the vision of God in the Book of Revelation. It is the Lamb who was slain who is accounted worthy to receive 'power and wealth and wisdom and might and honour and glory and blessing'.

The new beginning of the disciples in the Gospel is the same as Paul's, but different. Here are disciples who have known the Lord in his earthly life. Is Peter's decision to go fishing a sign of lack of faith, a desire to return to the old ways, a hankering for the days before the Lord came and interrupted his life, or is it motivated simply by the need to eat? Its importance in the story is that it sets up the possibility of an encounter with Jesus, and it provides the context in which Jesus shows himself to and renews his love and trust in Peter.

The language of John 21 is distinctive and provides strong grounds for the suggestion that this chapter is in some way additional to the rest of the Gospel. Moreover, language plays an important part in the conversation between Jesus and Peter, and it does this in two ways. First, the Greek uses two different words for love, and this is best reflected in J. B. Phillips' translation of this chapter. After breakfast, Jesus asks Simon Peter if he loves him, and Peter replies, 'Yes, Lord, You know that I am Your friend.' Jesus asks the question again, and again Peter replies, 'Yes, Lord, You know that I am Your friend.' The third time Jesus asks, 'Simon, son of John, *are* you my friend?' This is the cause of Peter's feeling 'deeply hurt', because Jesus' third question used Peter's own language – 'Are you my friend?' – and he replies using the same expression, 'You know that I am Your friend!'

The second way in which the language plays an important part mirrors the first, for Jesus also plays games with Peter's role as the leader of the Church by using different expressions in his conversation with Peter for the pastoral care which he will exercise – 'feed my lambs', 'care for my sheep,' and 'feed my sheep'.

On the one hand Peter determines the nature of his response, pursues his own purpose in the conversation, and that with some wit. On the other hand, Jesus shows his readiness to meet Peter's capacity for loving; it is as if he is saying, 'Two can play at that game; if you want to alter the words, that is fine, and I can do the same. What is important, however, is that the work of discipleship should be done and the flock of God must be cared for; I do not call for declarations of love greater than you are able to own.'

So both the completely new and the renewed have their place in

---

Interpretation

There are so many questions that could be asked of Easter and how it impinges on our lives. How seriously do we take it as the most important feast in the year? Do we celebrate it more lavishly than Christmas? What does it mean to walk today 'in newness of life', as St Paul puts it in Romans 6? How is this language from the first century, coloured as it is by the eschatological expectations of the day, to be understood in the light of our knowledge of the world today?

the mission of God; and both 'newnesses' have their origin in the resurrection of Jesus, with whom every day is a new beginning, every fall a new start, and every encounter an opportunity for conversation and deepening of the relationship.

Psalm 30 could have been written for these disciples. The misplaced zeal which led one to persecute and the other to deny or flee; the blindness which afflicted Paul in the process of his conversion; the sad resignation in Peter's 'I'm going fishing'; all these were grounds for self-questioning and confusion; but God, 'rich in mercy', restores them to life 'from among those gone down to the Pit'.

The Fourth Sunday of Easter

Acts 9:36–43; Psalm 23; Revelation 7:9–17; John 10:22–30

The reader of the Acts of the Apostles over these weeks may be struck by how the early Christian community lived the resurrection faith. The reference in this story to 'the saints and widows' suggests a community which has been in existence for a period of time, with some structure to their life. 'The saints' was a term for the whole community, and 'the widows' were probably those given the task of grieving with the families of the dead – much like the mourners in the story of Jairus' daughter in Luke 8:41ff.

This story echoes that and suggests that the Acts of the Apostles intends its readers to consider their life as punctuated by a repetition of the Easter story. Jairus' daughter was raised and, more importantly, just as Jesus was raised, so Tabitha is raised to life again in order to continue to serve the needs of God's people.

The other readings carry the theme of 'comfort' in adversity. In the case of Psalm 23 this is a general theme, but the others have the added sense of comfort in tribulation for disciples who suffer persecution. The seer in Revelation 7 has pointed out to him those 'which are come out of great tribulation', and John 10 speaks of the safety of those who are Jesus' sheep. That this part of the Gospel narrative takes place in winter adds significance to the protection that is offered to the sheep. They will not perish, because they are protected, both by the Son, who is the 'good shepherd', and by the Father, whose purpose is to keep faith with the Son.

The implication is, first, that tribulation is bound to come, but that, second, those who suffer will be consoled by Jesus himself and his Father. Few Christians in the West can be said to suffer much by way of 'tribulation' now. However, we do well to remember that many Christians in the past have done so, and that many still do in different parts of the world. We also know now that Christians have not only been persecuted, but have carried out persecutions; and we know too that people suffer unjustly simply for believing in something which is not acceptable to those in authority, or for acting on behalf of justice for those who suffer oppression.

Clearly, the point of the biblical exhortations to constancy is that God is on the side of his own people. The corollary today, as we consider who are God's people, must be that Christ is to be known in all the persecuted men, women and children around the world, and that God is on the side of the victims. A contemporary resurrection faith will suggest not simply that vindication comes to those who are Christians, but that God's purposes are focused in those who suffer for the cause of righteousness, and for those who are widowed and orphaned by the injustice of oppressors.

Interpretation

The question of justice and human rights is a lively one in contemporary society, and the Church has not always been on the side of the angels! There are those who fear that, if the Churches are too heavily involved in political activity, their message is reduced to a 'social gospel'. However, the call of Jesus Christ was always addressed to societies, and the implications of that call are for all human communities. Some of the earliest campaigners for human rights included Christians; and the realization that Christ is present especially in those who suffer is an important antidote to the notion that we are only concerned for a 'spiritual' salvation for the individual. The gospel is concerned with release from suffering for all who are oppressed; and the Church has much to learn from those who have no faith, but who are concerned to confront oppression and injustice, wherever it is to be found.

The Fifth Sunday of Easter

Acts 11:1–18; Psalm 148; Revelation 21:1–6; John 13:31–35

How wide is the love of God? Who is saved? Today's readings provide a pattern discernible in the Bible for an understanding of human salvation that gradually widens, till all people are included. The continuing story from the Acts of the Apostles is of Peter's defence of himself before the Church in Jerusalem after he has baptized Gentiles and thus admitted them to the Church. The story of Cornelius, according to Acts 10, had marked a watershed in the life of the early Christian community. Before that, the young Church had believed that belief in Jesus was simply one form of Jewish faith – of which there were several versions available. Peter's experience of God's leading convinced him, however, that Gentiles should also be admitted to faith. A little later, of course, Paul arrived on the scene and took an even more radical view of the implications for the whole human race of the life, death and resurrection of Jesus. Peter's account was accepted, we are told here, and the community gave thanks for God's ever-widening mercy, in that Gentiles were to be admitted to the fellowship of Christ's Church.

Thus the Bible marks the early stages of this development in Christian understanding, and provides some means of establishing criteria by which we construe what is compatible with faith in Christ. Here we see the beginnings of the development of the divine purpose of human salvation, through the chosen people of Israel, through the Church, through all people who respond, in sometimes unknown and hidden ways, to the God who is revealed in Christ.

Psalm 148 has the psalmist calling upon the whole creation to give thanks for the glory of God, especially in his commitment to his people in ensuring that they come through to vindication and glory after all their suffering. The image of 'a new heaven and a new earth' in Revelation 21 is central to such an understanding of the gospel – however judgmental earlier passages in the Book of Revelation have been. John the Seer's vision is of a totally newly created world, in which there is nothing to cause harm, nor anything to detract from a harmonious relationship with God. Here is an image of God's being 'all in all', and all the world being one in him, once inhuman and anti-human forces have been destroyed.

The same theme is present in today's Gospel. Jesus' exclamation, 'Now the Son of Man has been glorified, and God has been glorified in him,' occurs after Gentiles have approached the disciples with the desire to see Jesus. There is this thrust implicit in the Christian gospel for the uniting of the whole of humanity, and it is significant that such a weighty theological theme should issue, in John's Gospel, in Jesus giving a 'new commandment': that his followers should love one another. The unity which Christ desires and which is central to Christian preaching comes to expression in simple obedience; that those who take any note of him should live as he lived – in love. The glory of Christ is the love of people for one another. In that way they show that they have his Spirit.

Interpretation

How justified are we in seeing trends in the Bible, such as to an ever greater inclusiveness, and extrapolating from them to a completely universalist understanding of the gospel? Or does the Bible provide a blueprint for all the assertions which we must make about Christian faith, leaving us simply to quarry the text to extract its meaning? How far does God expect us to interact with the text and the culture of our own day, in order to discern how we must live out the faith in our own generation?

The Sixth Sunday of Easter

Acts 16:9–15; Psalm 67; Revelation 21:10,22–22:5; John 14:23–29
or John 5:1–9

Two Gospel readings are provided for today. The passage from
John 14 is prefaced by the question from Judas (not Iscariot, we
are told; this is no trick question from a future betrayer), 'Lord, how
is it that you will reveal yourself to us, and not to the world?' Jesus
appears to ignore the question and to speak of the love which is to
reign in the Christian community. He talks, too, of the peace which
he will leave as he departs from them. St John's Gospel, of course,
has no account of the Ascension, the festival which takes place this
coming week. When Jesus talks of his departure, then, he is referring
to his crucifixion and resurrection. These are the mystical means by
which he will be eternally present to his disciples. Since he will no
longer be physically present among them, it is important that they
remember the promise of his presence by the Spirit. We do well to
remember, however, that love within the Christian community and
the peace which he gives are spoken of in the context of a question
about the revelation of Jesus to the world; he is known in so far as he
is present in the love of those who confess him.

The reading from John 5 is about conflict: the words 'Now that
day was a sabbath', are the clue to that. The fact that the pool by the
Sheep Gate had five porticos suggests that it was constructed to
reflect the five books of the Law of Moses – the 'Pentateuch', as we
call the first five books of the Jewish scriptures. In Jewish tradition,
this Law taught the people how they were to conduct themselves – or
'walk', to use the metaphor which comes from the Hebrew word for
'way of life', *halakah*. After ensuring that the man who has been ill
for thirty-eight years himself puts into words his own need, Jesus
instructs him to take up his mat and 'walk'. The story proceeds with
the conflict that ensues as the man, cut loose from the 'walk' of his
former religious tradition, obeys the command of Jesus and gets into
trouble with those who are supposed to be guiding the people in their
walk before God. (There's a salutary lesson for all those of us who
claim to be teachers of the faith!)

In the order in which we read these lessons, the vision of new
Jerusalem sets the scene for this encounter of Jesus with the people

and authorities of the earthly Jerusalem. The nations are to 'walk' in the new holy city, and kings and peoples shall acknowledge its priority in glory and honour. The city is lit by the Lamb of God, and has need of no other light, so none will stumble; this will be home to all, and everything which would defile it is excluded.

In the Acts of the Apostles we come back to Philippi, the first city in which Paul preached the gospel in Europe. Here there was a prayer meeting, and a faithful woman who welcomed the apostles into her home. So a seller of purple cloth, the fabric of royalty, welcomes the ambassadors of the king of kings, and is numbered among those who will inherit and walk the streets of the city which is to come.

Interpretation

How might the notion of 'walking' be used today as a metaphor for Christian living and discipleship? Its use in Jewish tradition is interesting when put alongside the basic meaning of 'law', in Judaism, which is Torah, or 'direction'. There is a sense of movement in it, of progress towards a goal which is set before those who take this particular path.

Ascension Day

Acts 1:1–11 *or* Daniel 7:9–14; Psalm 47 *or* Psalm 93; Ephesians 1:15–23 *or* Acts 1:1–11; Luke 24:44–53

How do you tell the story of the end of the life of Jesus? Usually, the story of somebody's life ends with their death; however, the most important statement about Jesus is that he is not dead, but risen from the dead. Each evangelist tells his story differently. Mark's account hardly has a proper resurrection, because there are no appearances to disciples. Matthew and John describe him not going away at all, but, in ways that are neither explained nor explored, staying with the disciples and continuing, as the risen Son of God, to share their common life. Luke is the evangelist most committed to storytelling. He looks out for the causes and the effects of things, and makes theories and ideas into narratives.

Most of the best stories about Jesus come from Luke. The shepherds at his birth; the chorus of the angels; the stories of Elizabeth and Zechariah; some of the best known parables, such as the lost coin, the lost sheep and the prodigal son. What is more, Luke is the only evangelist to offer us a 'volume 2', the Acts of the Apostles, which carries the story of the followers of Jesus on into the life of the earliest churches.

For Luke, the life of Jesus consists in his preaching of the Kingdom of God, which includes all people in God's compassionate and barrier-free reign. Jesus' death represents the apparent triumph of the forces of evil, but in fact it is part of God's plan for the salvation of all, which begins with the raising of Jesus from the dead. The stories of Ascension and Pentecost are expansions of the resurrection story: they are particular types of resurrection appearances, the Ascension explaining why the resurrection appearances ended, and Pentecost saying how Jesus is still present to his disciples. Luke tells of the end of the appearances in order to show that Jesus has gone to share in the life of God.

So there is a second question: why were the disciples not sad when he left them? They are in John 16, but Luke seems more confident of what he is doing: that is, preparing the narrative ground for the story of the coming of the Spirit. The Ascension story is Luke's way of understanding the resurrection; it is not an absence, but it paves the way for a newly understood presence.

Luke's story says he goes away – as the story must, for the resurrection appearances of Jesus have stopped. But this is in order to make way for the story of the coming of the Spirit. This is not necessary in Matthew, for Jesus remains present. So in Luke there is a narrative paradox in order to allow for a theological statement. The point is, of course, that this is not a physical 'going' to another place, for God's home is not a place. God the Father lives everywhere by the Spirit. Jesus' 'going to the Father' necessarily implies and entails that his disciples 'go to the Father' with him – even though Luke tells this as having God come to them, as the Spirit. Hence the disciples' joy. They know that they are joined with Christ as he goes on to his future in the life of the Church. They also know that the Kingdom of God really has dawned among them. All people are now made one with Christ, 'outsiders' and all!

The Ascension of Jesus is the ascension of the whole of humanity to share in the life of God. That is the destiny of humankind; that is the presence of the kingdom of God, and that is what Christ brings about – he is both its means and its reality. This is cause for great thanksgiving and praise. So the Psalms we sing today are appropriately those of God's kingship, for it is a kingship in which Jesus shares, along with all who are called to reign with him.

Interpretation

What are the challenges in reinterpreting the first-century imagery of the Ascension story to our own day? How are we to address them? In what ways might they be met?

The Seventh Sunday of Easter

Acts 16:16–34; Psalm 97; Revelation 22:12–14,16–17,20–21;
John 17:20–26

In between the celebrations of Ascension and Pentecost, the Gospel draws our attention to what is commonly known as the 'High Priestly' prayer of Jesus in John 17. This remarkable composition contains a number of themes, and cannot be reduced simply to a proof text for ecumenism; its significance is even more important than that. It was penned, of course, before there were any structural divisions in the Church, so it represents a desire for a unity which is nothing to do with ecclesiastical organization. We do well to note that the model for the unity prayed for is that which exists between the Father and the Son – indeed, that which existed 'before the foundation of the world'. It also makes a particular reference to those who believe after the time of the apostles – and that includes us modern readers. (So it clearly originates in a time and place which no longer thought of the end of time as imminent!)

How is it to be understood? What is that unity which Jesus eternally enjoys with the Father? The word used in this passage is 'love'. What Jesus is praying for is therefore not 'Church unity', as we have come to understand and desire it, but rather 'Church continuity', a developed sense that those who believe today are at one with those who first believed at the preaching of Jesus himself and the apostles. That is not to say that faith and its formulation do not change; rather that we cannot understand our faith properly without a sense of its history and continuity with the belief of Christians of previous ages.

Elsewhere in John's Gospel the suggestion is made that the love between Jesus and the Father is evidenced in their wanting the same thing, in their working towards the same ends, in their having the same purpose. That purpose is the salvation of the world, and its effects are to be seen in the love which human beings have for one another. Those who have this hope find no difficulty in proclaiming, 'The Lord is king! Let the earth rejoice; let the many coastlands be glad!' Paul and Silas were singing the praises of God when the opportunity came to escape from prison in Philippi. Their refusal to do so led to the conversion of their jailer and his whole household. (They did not simply rejoice that the jailer had become a believer, as the New Revised Standard Version suggests; rather, the whole household was baptized.) The feast prepared for Paul and Silas was a precursor of the wedding breakfast of the Lamb to which all are invited who share in their passion for doing the will of God, both in the time of the apostles and today. The Book of Revelation finishes with the party to end all parties, for it celebrates all the joys of the Kingdom of God.

Interpretation

How is the faith of today to be understood in the light of its past? How must its formulation change? In what ways must it change in the light of change in the culture about us?

Day of Pentecost

Acts 2:1–21 *or* Genesis 11:1–9; Psalm 104:24–35b; Romans
8:14–17 *or* Acts 2:1–21; John 14:8–17, (25–27)

It seems that our prayers are frequently answered by all the ambi-
guity which met Philip's request for more specific information
about how Jesus relates to the Father. Why could Jesus not be more
specific? Maybe, like Philip, we are invited to look at the evidence
around us and decide whether the God who is the Father of Jesus is
worthy of worship. It would appear from this text that, in order to
be able to answer this, we have to commit ourselves to the loving
lifestyle of the God who is known to us in Jesus: 'If you love me, you
will keep my commandments, and I will ask the Father, and he will
give you another Advocate, to be with you forever. This is the Spirit
of truth . . .' Yet again, we are being told that to know God is to act
like God in love and compassion; we shall discover the Spirit of truth
as we live by the truth.

The lectionary is absolutely right to place the story of the Tower
of Babel alongside the story of Pentecost. Babel, or Babylon, of
course, stood for all that was evil in the eyes of Jewish tradition, and
the name of the city which dared to vie with God in glory was given
also to that prehistoric society representing a human race which
attempted to build a tower to reach to the heavens; there is a play on
the word *babel*, which has connotations of confusion, for the punishment for this presumption was the confusion of their language. The
Acts story reverses the judgment, and tells of nations formerly
divided by language now brought together by the Spirit of God: all
those visitors to Jerusalem heard the disciples speaking in their own
tongue. Luke's theological creativity brings these two stories together
and makes a point about the significance of language and speech,
especially with regard to the preaching of the good news of Jesus
Christ.

In the reading from Romans, Paul tells of the Spirit which is given
to Christian believers. This is none other, he says, than the Spirit
which is at work in creation; this is not some extra, special attribute
of God, but God at his creative work. There are no distinctions to be
drawn between the various works of God. God creates, God judges,
God reconciles; all is the work of the one God. It is the Spirit of God

who undertakes all that God wills, and it is the grace of God which underlies all God's actions. This Spirit makes us the children, the inheritors of the estate, of God. The one proviso is that we remember the cost of this grace to God, bearing in mind that what we suffer is also to be offered to the Father to be made holy, just as was the offering of Christ himself.

Application

What is our experience of living the Christian faith and noting that our desires are being conformed to the will of God? And how do we experience the power of language to create a world? There is an important connection between this question of self-awareness, and of the prior question about behaviour.

Trinity Sunday

Proverbs 8:1–4,22–31; Psalm 8; Romans 5:1–5; John 16:12–15

A familiar picture seen in a gallery or a favourite novel re-read –
both ask us to take a breathing space so that we can reassess
their impact. Trinity Sunday gives us the chance to take a step back
from the life story of Jesus of Nazareth, which we have been following for the last few months, and consider the difference which that
story has made to the way in which we view the world.

A tone of interconnectedness is set in the first reading from
Proverbs. 'Wisdom', in the biblical tradition, is not thought of
primarily as abstract knowledge or speculation, but as personal and
moral knowledge. To 'know God' is to recognize his authority and
live accordingly. Here 'wisdom' is a female principle who actively
seeks out those who will listen to her; who, like the Logos in John's
Gospel, reveals the secrets of God to those who will accept her.
Closely associated with the work of God in creation, she is the fulfilment of all 'natural' knowledge. If Jesus shows us the 'wisdom' of
God then we are reminded to look for him in mundane material.

The theme of a good and interconnected universe is continued in
Psalm 8. Stepping back from the picture shows us the broader
canvas, enabling us to see more of the grand design and to be awed
by the scale of it. If we are to see our calling to full humanity in the
life story of Jesus, then there is something here about perspective. In
the peculiarity and particularity of the apparently insignificant, the
majestic work of God goes on.

Paul, writing to the Romans, is anxious not to be misunderstood.
He believes that salvation is assured for those in Christ, but does not
believe that the resurrection life is yet attained in its fullness. On the
basis of God's gracious initiative much is achieved, and the life of the
Holy Spirit is poured out, but there is still work to be done and
Christians, humbled by their afflictions, are to put their trust in God
and not in themselves. As we step back from the grand canvas we
may be given a glimpse of how our own brushstrokes can be
incorporated – of how unlikely colours may yet be included. The life
story of Jesus has shown us that human limitation does not constrain
God.

The reading from John's Gospel is a reminder not to allow our images of God to become static. For this evangelist the Spirit is the Spirit of Truth – and 'truth' is one of his key words. Truth lies in the future and allows the possibility of some surprises yet to come. In this last gift of Jesus to his disciples we are encouraged to keep moving. If we continue to be his disciples, and from time to time to reassess the impact of his life story, we shall be gradually caught up in the dynamic of God's love and the whole picture will swirl with the divine life which he shows us.

Day of Thanksgiving for Holy Communion

Thursday after Trinity Sunday (Corpus Christi)

Genesis 14:18–20; Psalm 116:11-end; 1 Corinthians 11:23–26; John 6:51–58

Eating meals together – whether with family, friends or strangers – is the way we celebrate special events, remember times past, anticipate future projects, nourish our bodies and foster our relationships. Today's readings give us the opportunity to explore some of the meaning of the meal which Jesus inaugurated with his friends on the eve of the crucifixion. According to the earliest account in Paul's Letter to the Corinthians, the repetition of the story of his death is to continue in the Church 'until he comes'. Now, in the light of the resurrection and empowered by the gift of the Holy Spirit at Pentecost, we are to look at the implications of this charge.

The reading from Genesis takes us back to Abraham and to Melchizedek's blessing of him in the name of the creator god (El Elyon). In an unusual passage, which portrays the father of the nation as a military hero, we are reminded that the gifts of creation are to be held sacred, that physical things – bread and wine – may be means of blessing. Later tradition identified Salem with Jerusalem, the holy city and place of God's presence. The meal is about a peace agreement and nourishment received from God.

For Paul the memorial meal announces the beginning of the time of salvation. He looks forward to the Lord's return and understands this supper as an anticipation of the heavenly banquet of the Kingdom of God, an interim meal between the two comings of the Lord. He makes no reference here to the resurrection, which in his view does not essentially alter the situation. The Christian supper was founded on the sacrificial death of Jesus, an act of divine deliverance by which sins were forgiven and a new covenant set up between God and humanity. God's people must therefore be united amongst themselves. Paul has a stern rebuke for a Church which complacently imagines itself 'above' covenant responsibilities and beyond God's judgment. Judgment is still to come, ritual participation alone is not enough.

This point is made forcefully in the Gospel. A long chapter, describing the feeding of the five thousand and discussing bread from heaven, makes no overt reference to the Christian sacrament at all. The author is probably deliberate in not equating the Lord's Supper with salvation. He is more interested in the believer's loyalty to the Christian congregation, hence in the separation of the community from the world and its internal solidarity (for John's Church the issue may have been separation from the synagogue). Eternal life is certainly about participating in Christ's death, about interiorizing his life blood, but that is less to do with a Church ritual than with faith and mutual love and obedience to the end.

Background

Melchizedek, the King of Salem and priest of God most High, is a gloriously misty figure. His return is anticipated in the biblical material and, rather like King Arthur, he is not easily pinned to a historical background. Generally the Palestine of the patriarchal stories fits best somewhere in the Middle Bronze Age (between the twentieth and sixteenth centuries BCE) when semi-nomadic groups were gradually beginning to settle down in that part of the world. In our story Abram paid tithes to Melchizedek, acknowledging his superiority. King David apparently tried to appropriate his royal and sacerdotal power (Psalm 110:4). The author of Hebrews argues that Jesus is a priest for ever 'after the order of Melchizedek' (Hebrews 5:6,10; 6:20; 7:17) and in one of the Dead Sea Scrolls (1 Q Melch.) Melchizedek is a heavenly being who will bring salvation and judgment at the conclusion of the final jubilee. He features in Gnostic literature – and in the Slavonic version of 2 Enoch (first century CE) a new Melchizedek will arise, in the last generation, greater than all his predecessors, to work miracles and rule as king and priest.

Ordinary Time – Proper 4

Sunday between 29 May and 4 June

1 Kings 18:20–21,30–39 *or* 20–39 *with* Psalm 96; *or* 1 Kings 8:22–23,41–43 *with* Psalm 96; Galatians 1:1–12; Luke 7:1–10

We begin today a selection of passages from Galatians, possibly Paul's earliest letter. And we pick up again the consecutive reading of Luke's Gospel. We are vividly reminded by 1 Kings 8:41–43 that, even in Old Testament times, God was concerned for all peoples on earth – something beautifully celebrated in today's Psalm; while the story of Elijah in 1 Kings 18 raises acutely the question of the nature of faith. Both these themes are taken up in the New Testament readings.

Galatians is probably addressed to the Gentile congregations founded on Paul's first missionary journey, recorded in Acts 13–14. If so, they are his first missionary babies! So he cares for them passionately, fiercely denouncing those who are disturbing them and trying to distort the gospel of Christ. We discover the problem later; some Jewish Christian missionaries had followed Paul to these Churches, and tried to persuade them to accept circumcision as Jews. Verse 10 probably reflects their accusation of Paul – that he was toning down the demands of the gospel in order to 'please' the Galatians.

We will trace Paul's arguments against them in the coming weeks. Here at the start, like Elijah on Mount Carmel, he simply faces them with his claim – that his gospel is the true one, directly revealed to him by God. Verses 1 and 12 refer to his vision of Christ on the Damascus Road (Acts 9).

The Gospel reading points us toward one of the arguments Paul will develop in Galatians. Jesus' words about the centurion are truly remarkable: although a Gentile, he has greater faith than any Jew Jesus has met. Luke does not spell out how this can be, but later he introduces us to another centurion, Cornelius (Acts 10), who likewise exercises faith in Jesus, and then dramatically receives the Holy Spirit, without being circumcised as a Jew, to show that now God shows no partiality (Acts 10:34). God has broken down the age-long distinction between Jews and Gentiles and accepts everyone simply on the basis of faith, and not because of adherence to any nationality, religion or law.

But Cornelius comes later. Here Luke prepares the way by enabling us to see some of the universal features of faith illustrated by this centurion. First, faith focuses upon Christ rather than on human need. Though deeply concerned about his servant, the centurion is moved primarily by his remarkable awareness of Jesus' inbuilt authority. Second, faith forces a new self-assessment. The elders call him worthy, and doubtless he was, but he measures

Theology

Elijah on Mount Carmel, Paul's polemics against the 'Judaisers', the centurion, and Cornelius in Acts 10 all raise the question of salvation outside Christ: can it be? This is a question of great importance in today's pluralistic world, and these readings seem to pull in opposite directions. On the one hand Elijah and Paul require a black and white decision. Israel must renounce Baal and his priests, and worship the Lord alone. And the Galatians must recognize that God's curse rests on any who preach a different gospel from Paul's. But on the other hand the centurion, and Cornelius, already exercise great faith, before meeting or hearing of Christ, and Peter's comment about Cornelius is that 'in every nation anyone who fears God and does what is right is acceptable to him' (Acts 10:35).

It is tempting to say that these two Roman soldiers illustrate Karl Rahner's concept of 'the anonymous Christian': that is, people who can be regarded as 'in Christ', and who thus attain salvation in him, though their status in him has not yet become a conscious faith for them. It is tempting, because Rahner's concept is attractive in an age in which exclusive claims for any religion are not politically correct.

himself differently: 'I did not judge myself worthy to come to you.' The standard of measurement is Jesus, not social approval. Third, faith responds to Jesus' word. Luke places this story straight after the 'Sermon on the Plain' (6:20–49). So when the centurion says, 'Only speak the word . . .,' we realize that he cannot have this word (of healing) without having all Jesus' other words as well – as indeed Jesus himself makes clear, for he makes preaching the gospel and healing a single, two-pronged ministry (see Luke 4:18).

This is the faith which Jesus calls 'great'!

Rahner's view was based on an anthropology which emphasized our capacity to know God, and critics have argued that he did not take sufficient account of the Fall, and of the effects of sin on our knowing, as well as on our behaving. It is certainly true that, in the New Testament, knowledge of God is only possible for a transformed mind, that is, one which has been renewed in conscious dependence on Christ and the Holy Spirit (for example, Matthew 11:25–30; John 17; 1 Corinthians 2:7–16; Ephesians 1:16–19). This is chiefly because this kind of knowledge is relational rather than solely rational, and it is hard to conceive of a relationship which shapes our being and our knowing, and yet of which the knower is unconscious.

So even Cornelius needs to hear of and respond to Christ, that is, to grasp intellectually, and then relationally through the Spirit, that Christ is the one through whom God is truly known and worshipped. The period before his conversion, therefore, is pictured as a time of searching rather than of finding. And maybe this helps us forward theologically: for searching need not be far from finding, and those who seek may already grasp much of the truth (see Mark 12:28–34). Christians can fully recognize this, and yet maintain that 'only in Christ is the veil taken away' (2 Corinthians 3:14).

Ordinary Time – Proper 5

Sunday between 5 and 11 June

1 Kings 17:8–16 *or* 8–24 *with* Psalm 146; *or* 1 Kings 17:17–24 *with* Psalm 30; Galatians 1:11–24; Luke 7:11–17

Today's readings gather around the themes of prophets and faith, and raise fascinating and challenging questions for our time. Elijah lives by obedience to the word of God, and the widow of Zarephath learns to do this too, even through great pain. When she sees her son alive again, she accepts that Elijah is a true prophet: 'Now I know that you are a man of God, and that the word of the Lord in your mouth is truth.'

Something similar happens when Jesus also raises a widow's son. The crowd reacts by calling him a prophet – in fact, 'A great prophet has risen among us! God has visited his people!' (Luke 7:16). Why do they draw this conclusion? The answer lies in their understanding of the word of God. A 'prophet' speaks the words of God in a particular way. They once called the world into being: 'And God said, "Let there be light," and there was light' (Genesis 1:3). Prophetic words thus have creative power, power even to raise the dead. When the crowd calls Jesus a great prophet, they are identifying him as the prophet promised by Moses in Deuteronomy 18:15: 'The Lord your God shall raise up for you a prophet like me from among your own people; you shall heed such a prophet!' So God's word as power cannot be separated from God's word as instruction, and the crowd realizes they must listen to, and obey, this great prophet now revealed before them.

Authentic Christian faith, we learn, is marked by obedience to the words of God as spoken by Jesus Christ. It is essentially something practical, rather than cerebral: a confession, followed by a reformation.

But prophets are not always proved by words of power in this way. In the Galatians passage Paul claims strongly to be a prophet: his description of his call is deliberately comparable to Jeremiah's (Jeremiah 1:5). He insists on it, because opponents were suggesting that his gospel was his own invention, in independence of the truly authoritative Jerusalem apostles. 'Oh no!' Paul replies, 'I did not have much contact with Jerusalem, it is true, but I did not avoid

Background

The relationship between Paul and the Church in Jerusalem was rather fraught. In today's passage Paul asserts his independence of the other apostles, perhaps in bold *acceptance* of the charge that his gospel was in some respects different from that preached at Jerusalem. In the next chapter, as we will see, Paul was upfront about his disagreement with the pressure from Jerusalem, to which Peter submitted. But he *insists* that, though different, his gospel was given to him directly by God himself, in the revelation of Christ on the Damascus Road.

It is not surprising, therefore, that Jewish Christians in Jerusalem were deeply suspicious of Paul. Luke records their attitude in Acts 21:20–21: they thought that Paul was a dangerous lawbreaker who drove a wedge between Jesus and Moses. In Galatians we hear Paul speak on this topic in his own words, and can judge whether that charge is true or not!

At any rate, having asserted his independence of Jerusalem, Paul next (equally boldly) asserts his agreement with Jerusalem on the essential gospel (Galatians 2:1–10). His opponents may have found this incredible. But Paul himself clearly believed that the leaders of the Jerusalem Church accepted both him and his law-free gospel, not requiring any changes, but affirming the *de facto* separation of spheres of operation (Galatians 2:7–9).

The 'men from James', therefore, who caused the trouble in Antioch (see Galatians 2:12), must, in Paul's view, have misrepresented James when they insisted that the Jewish food laws should still apply in Christian fellowship. Whether they misrepresented him or not, it is important for us to be aware of the theological and practical issues at stake in the tense debate between Paul and the 'Jerusalem' gospel – because finally Paul won the argument, and we today assume without question that (to put it sharply) we do not need to become Jews in order to be Christians. This was by no means agreed, in the earliest years of the Church.

them. I did not go, because I did not need to; God had revealed his Son to me without intermediary.'

The interesting thing is that Paul does not appeal to any words of power he had uttered to prove his prophetic status. He had performed some miracles in the Galatian Churches, according to Acts (14:3), and he refers to these later (Galatians 3:5). But he does not mention them here. Why not?

Probably because true faith never rests on proof. The widow of Zarephath had to trust that Elijah was a true prophet before ever her son was restored to life: see the story of how she made a snack for him! The grieving widow and the pall-bearers did not resist Jesus' approach, but willingly stopped the funeral procession for him. Faith receives its confirmation after the point of no return, and not before. Words of power from God are heard with the ears of faith.

Both stories are concerned with death. And in facing death – as Psalm 30 so eloquently shows – faith cannot seek proof before committing itself to trust in the power of Christ.

Ordinary Time – Proper 6

Sunday between 12 and 18 June

1 Kings 21:1–10,15–21a *or* 1–21a *with* Psalm 5:1–8; *or*
2 Samuel 11:26–12:10,13–15 *with* Psalm 32; Galatians 2:15–21;
Luke 7:36–8:3

Today's readings bring vividly before us the extravagant forgiveness and grace of God. The playground cry 'That's not fair!' expresses a principle of justice that governs human relationships in all civilized societies. We expect to be treated fairly by the law, and by our fellow human beings. So it can be difficult to take on board the realization that unfairness is at the heart of the Christian gospel.

But of course Paul does not put it like that. He calls it 'justification by faith', and this Galatians passage is a most important summary-statement of his teaching about this. The point is: God does not measure us against a list of rules, so as to decide whether or not we qualify for heaven. The result of this would be disastrous: 'No one will be justified by the works of the Law' (Galatians 2:16b). So God refuses to give us what we deserve, and, against justice, justifies us through Christ.

David experiences this dramatically in Nathan's amazing assurance, 'The Lord has taken away your sin' (2 Samuel 12:13). Justice would demand the penalty for a murderer, but David is spared. The sinful woman in the Gospel passage should be sent packing with the rebuke which Simon the Pharisee clearly has in mind, but, instead, she experiences love, acceptance and forgiveness from Jesus, and comes away feeling, no doubt, that Jesus prizes her, in spite of her sexually charged action which offends Simon so deeply. Jesus sees her heart, and mediates forgiveness to her. Such forgiveness and acceptance are celebrated in Psalm 32, 'Blessed are those whose sin the Lord does not count against them' (verse 2).

The condition of such acceptance is simply confession. David could have blustered with Nathan, and continued the cover-up. But instead he came clean: 'I have sinned against the Lord.' The woman was ready publicly to renounce her sinful lifestyle, and to risk public shame in order to get to Jesus. The psalmist reminds himself of the agony when he tried to keep silent about his sin (verse 3).

As soon as he acknowledged it, forgiveness was immediately there.

Paul looks at this from a challenging angle in Galatians 2. If God simply 'justifies' us like this, then religion can actually be a hindrance, rather than a help. Paul had given up his Judaism, with its emphasis on scrupulous observance of lifestyle rules, festivals and prayer-times, because he realized that it was incompatible with faith. This seems extraordinary. But he knew that, in the long run, religion alone has nothing to offer social outcasts like the woman of Luke 7. And indeed he had discovered – horror of horrors – that his religion had actually led him to persecute God's Messiah. So when Peter tried to reintegrate religion into Christian faith, Paul was horrified again and opposed the great apostle publicly (Galatians 2:11–14).

Religious observance can cushion us against a realistic encounter with God, with our eyes open to our sinfulness before him. Simon the Pharisee warns us, and the weeping woman encourages us. To whom will we listen?

Ordinary Time – Proper 7

Sunday between 19 and 25 June

1 Kings 19:1–4, 8–15a *or* 1–15a *with* Psalms 42–43; *or* Isaiah 65:1–9 *with* Psalm 22:19–28; Galatians 3:23–29; Luke 8:26–39

Today's readings are designed to give hope to the hopeless. The Gospel passage introduces us to a complete no-hoper, a poor man whose mind is so deranged that he lives naked in a graveyard, isolated from all normal human contact. We can only imagine the pain and the slow loss of hope felt by his friends and relatives, as for a long time they had tried to rescue him in vain. He symbolizes for us all such people, so victimized by powers within them – physical, emotional, mental or even demonic – that they are condemned to a half-life, imprisoned within the thick walls of their incapacity.

Out of the boat steps Jesus, and with him a power which by a word is able to restore this poor man. It doesn't often happen like that, but Christians believe in a Saviour who can deliver such people and who anyway draws close, unlike those who abandoned this man to the uncleanness of the graveyard. This hope has sustained many a carer through long days and nights of selfless labour.

The Psalms (42 and 43 – originally one Psalm) introduce us to the inside of such an experience. The writer is crippled by depression. He remembers the time when he was filled with joy in worship (42:4), but it seems like another world. Now he has been washed away by a torrent (42:7). But even in his depression he reaches out in hope to God, for he knows that his condition is abnormal, and that God who is a rock (42:9) and stronghold (43:2) will one day restore his capacity for joy and delight (43:4). Even within depression, hope is possible, for it rests on reading sorrow as longing for something better (42:1–2).

In the case of Elijah (1 Kings 19) we see another such experience. In his case the depression is reactive: he has just had an amazing spiritual 'high' on Mount Carmel, where he has seen the power of God at work in a highly dramatic way. Suddenly – possibly because of tiredness and overconfidence – his feelings collapse, he cannot cope with Jezebel's challenge, and he ends up alone and suicidal in the desert. But God steps in with hidden sustenance and takes him away for a rest-cure on Mount Horeb. It takes time, but eventually he is back again.

Paul reminds us that, by nature, we are all prisoners, held prisoners by the Law because of our incapacity to obey this statement of God's will. God's Law, he says elsewhere, is 'holy, righteous and good' (Romans 7:12), and condemns all who are less than that. But there is hope – for those who simply reach out in faith, like the

---

Theology

Passages like today's reading from Galatians convinced Paul's opponents that they were right to charge him with gross 'law-lessness', because he actually says that believers in Jesus Christ 'are no longer subject' to the law (Galatians 3:25). How could this be right? This is the Law of God!

But Paul is uncompromising in his insistence that *God himself* has brought the era of the law to an end.

Paul's fundamental argument for this is summarized in Galatians 2:21: 'If justification comes through the law, then Christ died for nothing'. Here he gives us a window into his wrestling to understand his encounter with Christ on the Damascus Road. To his amazement, he discovered that, after all, this crucified and accursed figure *is* the Messiah. So the question, 'Why did the Messiah die?' became acute and urgent for him. It seems that, very quickly, Paul came to see the death of the Messiah as *atoning* – that is, as a death *for others* and *for sin*. He may have adopted this view from the Christians he joined on his conversion, or he may have argued through to it himself as he sought *reasons* for the Messiah's death.

But if the death of the Messiah was necessary in order to atone for sin, then clearly the law was not sufficient to do this. For Paul, the law *included* the sacrificial cult centred on Jerusalem, through which he had always believed that atonement for sin was made. Suddenly, he realized that the cult could not have been the answer. But what then *was* the

---

demoniac on the beach whose very ravings were a prayer for deliverance, and like the psalmist and Elijah, who cast themselves on God in their dejection. Such faith by itself, says Paul, turns slaves into heirs and heiresses liable to inherit Abraham's fortune through Christ (Galatians 3:29).

None of the greatest sinners, nor any of the most complete no-hopers, are beyond the capacity of God to touch and heal.

---

purpose of the law, if it was *not* to atone for sin and to preserve Israel in the ways of righteousness?

He answers this question in today's reading (Galatians 3:24–25) by describing the law as a 'disciplinarian' (NRSV) or 'custodian' (RSV) or 'tutor' (NEB): he uses the word which referred to the slave put in charge of taking the children of the household to school. This 'guardian' had to deliver them safely there, and then bring them home again. So the law guards us and delivers us safely into the arms of Christ, he suggests.

Martin Luther thought that the law discharged this function by revealing our sinfulness – so that, condemned by our inability to keep the law, we would realize our need of another Saviour, Jesus. However, in all probability Paul was thinking more broadly than this, because for him 'the law' is the whole Old Testament revelation, not just the moral law which we cannot obey.

So by his view of the law as a 'guardian to lead us to Christ', Paul lays the foundation for the Christian use of the Old Testament which has been a central tradition of the Church throughout its history – and underlies our lectionary, with its twinning of Old and New Testament readings and its incorporation of the Psalms into Christian worship. Far from rejecting the law totally (which some of his followers favoured), Paul found a way in theory of holding law and gospel together around the person of Christ, thus inviting us to read the Old Testament christologically. How to do that in practice, of course, is something we are still discovering!

Ordinary Time – Proper 8

Sunday between 26 June and 2 July

2 Kings 2:1–2,6–14 *with* Psalm 77:1–2,11–20; *or* 1 Kings
19:15–16,19–21 *with* Psalm 16; Galatians 5:1,13–25; Luke 9:51–62

The Epistle reading from Galatians 5 unpacks the meaning of Christian freedom by contrasting the works of the flesh (verses 19–21) with the fruit of the Spirit (verse 22). Paul knew that it was just as possible for Christian people, as for anyone else, to bite and devour each other (verse 15) by indulging in impulsive sex, drunkenness, jealousy, arguing, violent outbursts, selfish ambition, rivalry and division (verses 20–21) – collector's items from the Human Foibles Exhibition, on display up every street and in every soap opera.

But the Gospel reading reveals how the nicest people can become trapped by history into an ossified relationship of official hostility out of which they cannot break. The Samaritans refuse hospitality to Jesus and his disciples, and then in righteous indignation James and John propose an appropriately hostile response. Out of the highest religious motives, the works of the flesh are given full rein. How do you escape from them? It takes the radical action of Jesus, who simply passes through quietly, absorbs the hatred and accepts the homelessness (verse 58). He thus displays at least five segments of the fruit of the Spirit!

In the sayings which follow Jesus turns the incident into a pattern of discipleship. Behind 'the works of the flesh' lies the desire to possess, to be recognized as right, to have status and power. The disciples of Jesus must lay down all this, and be ready to accept homelessness with their Lord. Jesus demands of us a loyalty greater than that to our closest and dearest relatives (verse 60).

Does Jesus mean this literally? Elsewhere he criticizes people strongly for evading their responsibility to their parents (Mark 7:9–13). Sayings like Luke 9:60 are known as 'focal instances' (see the comment on Luke 6:28–30 for Proper 3, p 44 above), that is, Jesus' radical demand on us, his disciples, is focused by showing what it *could* mean. Following him is more important even than having a home and caring for elderly parents. Of course, he may permit us to have possessions, and may *command* us to care for elderly parents, but this central demand overrides all else: go and proclaim the Kingdom of God, in and through all you do!

The parallel with the story of the call of Elisha in 1 Kings 19 brings out the significance of proclaiming the Kingdom of God. Just as Elijah appointed Elisha to succeed him as prophet, so Jesus appoints his followers to a prophetic ministry before the world: 'Proclaim the Kingdom!' Elisha instinctively knew what this meant. Without hesitation, he sacrificed his most prized possession, the twelve yoke of oxen for which doubtless he was a local celebrity, and thus dramatically severed his connection with his past life.

The fruit of the Spirit can be very costly to produce. The tree needs to be well manured by burying under it all those possessions, ambitions and desires which might otherwise produce very different works. Those who belong to the Christ, Paul tells us, have crucified

---

Text

Luke 9:55–56 is one of those rare places where the Greek text of the New Testament contains substantial variants, that is, differences between manuscripts. The science of 'textual criticism' was developed during the nineteenth century in response to the discovery of many more New Testament manuscripts (now totalling over five thousand part or whole texts). Scholars have developed highly sophisticated methods of determining which 'reading' was the original, although in some places certainty is still impossible.

In this instance there is little doubt that the shorter text is the original, although most translations include the longer versions of verses 55–56 in a footnote: '[Turning to them he rebuked them,] and said, "You do not know what kind of spirit you are of, for the Son of Man did not come to destroy people's lives, but to save them." [And they went to another village].' The additional section is included in a group of manuscripts associated, originally, with the town of Caesarea and with the ministry of Origen, the third-century Church father. It is just possible that Origen has preserved for us an original saying of Jesus which has been incorporated into the text of Luke at this point.

the flesh with its passions and desires (Galatians 5:24). The challenge of these readings is very sharp: if Christ calls, are we ready to sacrifice all for him?

Ordinary Time – Proper 9

Sunday between 3 and 9 July

2 Kings 5:1–14 *with* Psalm 30; *or* Isaiah 66:10–14 *with*
Psalm 66:1–9; Galatians 6:7–16 *or* 1–16; Luke 10:1–11,16–20

The theme of mission links today's readings. The seventy-two
disciples were thrown into the deep end by Jesus, no doubt feeling like lambs among wolves (Luke 10:3) as they went out without
even basic equipment for travelling. The point was to make them
walking advertisements for the truth they were proclaiming, the
presence of the Kingdom. If God could heal the sick through their
hands, then he would surely protect and provide for them. Giving
hospitality to these messengers, therefore, meant becoming part of
their mission and entering the peace which they brought from God
(verse 6).

Not all mission adopts this method, but the principle of the walking advertisement is essential. We see it in Paul, although in fact he
followed a very different pattern. He refused to accept hospitality
from the people he travelled to, and insisted on supporting himself.
But the reason he gave made this an advertisement, also: the gospel
was good news, and he wanted to preach it free of charge (1
Corinthians 9:14–18).

Not everyone will be called to travelling mission like this. But we
can all *look outwards,* says Paul in the Epistle reading: 'While we
have opportunity, let us do good to all, particularly to those who
belong to the household of faith' (verse 10). He warns the Galatians
against a bad way of doing mission, exemplified in his opponents,
who had been trying to persuade the Galatians to be circumcised:
'They want you to be circumcised, so that they may boast in your
flesh!' (verse 13). Scalp-hunting is bad mission. But Paul himself
modelled a different way. He was so in love with Jesus Christ, and so
aware of the new creation which he had experienced through Christ,
that he could not keep silent about the cross, he must *boast* about it
(verses 14–15). He speaks the peace of the missionary on all who will
live by this rule (verse 16).

For many of us, opportunities are as limited as they were for the
little Israelite slave-girl who served Naaman's wife. How much does

a slave count in the affairs of nations? But she knew what she knew, and did not keep silent, because she loved the people she served, even though they had wrenched her away from her own family and country: 'If only my master would see the prophet who is in Samaria! He would cure him of his leprosy' (verse 3). Her integrity and genuineness shone so brightly that the great commander believed her and set off, willing to spend a fortune. She was a walking advertisement.

We can start by reaching out to each other, bearing one another's burdens, to 'fulfil the law of Christ' (Galatians 6:2). But when we have learned to do that, there is a world of need waiting to feel our touch as we reach out in the name of Christ, whose cross can bring such hope in darkness. The world still needs such walking advertisements of his faith and love, people inspired by the vision of Isaiah 66 – of a world drawn out of hostility into comfort and love by the call of God in Christ.

Ordinary Time – Proper 10

Sunday between 10 and 16 July

Amos 7:7–17 *with* Psalm 82; *or* Deuteronomy 30:9–14 *with* Psalm 25:1–10; Colossians 1:1–14; Luke 10:25–37

Alongside the continuing series from Luke, this Sunday sees the beginning of two new series of readings: a set of four from Colossians, and a series from Amos, Hosea and Jeremiah which will last to the end of the Trinity season.

In the first of two readings from Amos, we meet the rustic prophet causing a rumpus at the high-society royal sanctuary at Bethel, where he denounces its pompous religiosity. The parable of the Good Samaritan is more gently expressed, but no less cutting in its attack on 'religion', as we shall see below.

In the powerful opening verses of Colossians, Paul first gives thanks for his readers' faith (verses 3–8), and then prays for them (verses 9–14). In both cases the report of his prayer expands into comments, in the first case about the spread of the gospel (verses 6–8), and in the second case about the reasons for thanksgiving (verses 12–14). His prayer is full of Old Testament and Jewish language and ideas. He uses the language of Israel as he gives thanks for their faith, their love for all the saints, and their hope focused on heaven, and as he prays that they may know God's will, please him in every good work and give thanks to the Father who has given them an inheritance and brought them into his Kingdom by redemption and forgiveness of sin.

These ideas were all Jewish, but the Colossian believers were probably mainly Gentiles. Here is Paul praying that they may fully enjoy the relationship with God which Israel was supposed to have. On what basis does Paul transfer this relationship to Gentiles? This is a long and complicated story which takes us to the heart of Paul's theology, but we see the way being paved by passages like the parable of the Good Samaritan.

Contrary to popular belief, the parable does not simply mean, 'Do good to your neighbour.' It also says more than, 'Do your best to show compassion across barriers of racial hostility, like that between Jews and Samaritans.' The point is that it is the impure Samaritan sinner who fulfils the will and love of God, while the priest and Levite fail to do so, precisely because of their deep passion for God. They avoid the wounded man, not because they do not care, but because they will be disqualified from their temple duties if they handle a corpse. So their desire for purity leads them into dis-obedience, while the Samaritan's disregard of such issues enables him to obey the first command of the Law (Deuteronomy 6:5), recited morning and evening by every Jew.

The parable of the Good Samaritan thus paves the way for the worldwide gospel in which Paul rejoices (Colossians 1:6). The vital thing is the orientation of the heart toward God. If the heart is right, then detailed regulations become unimportant – even things com-manded in the Law. In fact, the Law says this too, as we see in the read-ing from Deuteronomy 30. 'God's word is not a distant prize, but very near you . . . in your mouth and in your heart so that you may obey it.' When Paul quotes this passage in Romans 10:6–10, he makes it very clear that it is through Christ alone that the heart is re-created for obe-dience in this way. And this re-creation is now possible for *all* through the power of the Spirit – not just for Jews. Paul give thanks that he has actually seen it in the faith, hope and love displayed by the Colossians.

Background

Amos is probably the earliest of the 'canonical' prophets, that is, those whose oracles have been preserved in written form. He prophesied during the reign of Jeroboam, king of Israel, whose long reign (783–743 BCE) brought great prosperity to the northern kingdom. But Amos actually came from Tekoa in Judah, the separated southern kingdom, which would in itself have made it difficult for him to gain a hearing in the north, quite apart from the obstacle of his rural origins (7:14). Tribal and social snobbery oozes out of Amaziah's rejection of him in 7:12.

Amos's prophecy concentrates on the abuses of religion at the royal sanctuary in Bethel, where religiosity went hand in hand with social injustice. He was fired with a burning sense of the coming judgment of God – which fell not long afterwards, through an invasion by the Assyrians in 721 BCE.

Ordinary Time – Proper 11

Sunday between 17 and 23 July

Amos 8:1–12 *with* Psalm 52; *or* Genesis 18:1–10a *with* Psalm 15; Colossians 1:15–28; Luke 10:38–42

There is an interesting balance between the Gospel reading and the story of Abraham and his visitors in Genesis 18. Martha is gently rebuked by Jesus for thinking that hospitality is more important than listening to his teaching. But on the other hand, it was through being hospitable that Abraham got to hear God's word for him and Sarah. Ordinary things like cooking or working can either distract us and block the Spirit, or form a channel and opportunity for the Spirit. What makes the difference?

The difference appears when we ask what really grips and fires our imagination. Imagination creates longing, and fuels desire. It is fundamental to our make-up as human beings. C. S. Lewis called it joy, as he attempted to name that inarticulate yearning which sometimes wells up inside us.

Of course, it can be corrupt. Our imagination can be sparked in this way by bad objects and desires. In Psalm 52 we meet the man who plots destruction, who loves evil more than good, above all who trusts in abundant riches, and seeks refuge in wealth. Similarly in the Amos passage we meet wheeler-dealers who cheat the poor by increasing the weights on their market scales, by adding dust to the wheat they sell, and by slightly reducing the size of the standard measure, the *ephah*. They long for festival days and sabbaths to end, so that they can get back to trading. Their imagination is gripped and drawn by money. That is the way of disaster and ruin, Amos tells his hearers. In the long run, the capacity to receive anything better is destroyed: people will want to hear God, but they simply will not be able to. The picture in Amos 8:12 points to a society adrift, desperately seeking something beyond the merely material, but unable to find it.

This all helps us to understand Jesus' words to Martha. Hospitality is of course important, and Mary understood this as much as her sister. But Mary was consumed with such a desire to listen to Jesus, that her sense of propriety as a hostess went out of the window! She could not tear herself away. She was gripped. For Martha, on the other hand, love for Jesus meant serving him a meal. Jesus gently tells her that feeding the spirit is more important than feeding the body.

That is the difference between Martha and Abraham. Abraham was the friend of God (Isaiah 41:8, James 2:23). The priority of his relationship with God was absolute. Martha's horizons were much smaller. For her, the ordinary blocked the Spirit. For him, it could not.

The size of our horizons will be measured by the reading from Colossians: a magnificent presentation of Jesus Christ (probably an early hymn, in fact) which appeals first and foremost to the imagination rather than the intellect. Intellect follows along behind, asking questions, but imagination or joy goes on ahead, prompting adoration of this Christ who is before all things, and in whom all things are reconciled to God. Do we long to know this Christ above all else?

Ordinary Time – Proper 12

Sunday between 24 and 30 July

Hosea 1:2–10 *with* Psalm 85; *or* Genesis 18:20–32 *with* Psalm 138; Colossians 2:6–15 *or* 6–19; Luke 11:1–13

Today's readings present us, in different ways, with the challenge of engagement with the world. The temptation to withdraw into spiritual comfort has always been alluring; but the Fathers of the monastic tradition quickly realized that God was actually calling them to a different form of engagement, not to withdrawal. We will see what this is, as we reflect on these passages.

In Colossians the engagement is ideological – that is, it concerns ideas. Paul wants the Church in Colossae to 'live in Christ . . . rooted and built up in him and established in the faith, just as you were taught'. Paul knew that there were many philosophical and religious ideas in the air at Colossae: in fact, religious syncretism (combining ideas from different sources) was very common, and Paul knew that the gospel could easily be watered down with inputs from paganism or Judaism. He urges them to understand how God's fullness dwells in Christ, so that they need not incorporate bits of other religions into their faith. In today's pluralistic world, the gospel makes the same unique claim upon us.

In Hosea the engagement is much more personal and direct. God calls his prophet to marry a prostitute, so as to experience for himself the pain of rejection which God felt at the unfaithfulness of his people. This prophetic act spoke volumes to Hosea's contemporaries (whether they heard or not): God is as involved with his people as if he were married to them. Occasionally we hear talk about the prophetic role of the Church in today's society. If Hosea is our model, then we will not assume such a role until we are deeply involved, tasting its bitterness and sharing its pain – or, more precisely, God's pain – at the twistedness of people's lives.

Abraham too was a prophet. God revealed to him the coming destruction of Sodom, where Abraham's nephew Lot was living. So Abraham prays for the city, clearly with Lot especially in mind. But he does not pray that God will save Lot from the destruction, but that the city may be saved because of the presence of Lot and his family. This is why the prayer is so tentative: Abraham is asking God to change his mind.

What impudence! But actually Jesus encourages us to be impudent in prayer in the Gospel reading, like the man who impudently wakes up his neighbour late at night to ask for bread. The word translated 'persistence' in Luke 11:8 means more literally 'shamelessness' or 'impudence'. The point is that he wants the bread for others, and to such prayer Jesus attaches the extravagant promise of verses 9–10. Why, you can even ask God for the Holy Spirit (verse 13) – an unthinkably impudent request for first-century Jews! – and he will answer, if you ask so that you may serve others.

The ministry of prayer is an engagement with the needs of the world: the monastic tradition of the Church reminds us how vital this is. But we do not have to join a religious order to take up this ministry. By the power of the Spirit, right now we can imitate the impudence of Abraham in pleading with God for this suffering and distracted world.

Interpretation

The question of whether Hosea's narrative reflects real episodes in the life of the prophet – or is an allegory – has provoked disagreement since ancient times. Modern commentators tend to the view that the very nature of prophetic symbolism means that the divine word must be actualized in real events. Most likely Hosea chose his wife from amongst the sacred prostitutes of the Ba'al cult – someone who had herself 'played the harlot' in what the prophets denounced as the 'harlotry' of Israel.

Ordinary Time – Proper 13

Sunday between 31 July and 6 August

Hosea 11:1–11 *with* Psalm 107:1–9,43; *or* Ecclesiastes 1:2,12–14; 2:18–23 *with* Psalm 49:1–12; Colossians 3:1–11; Luke 12:13–21

Luke's Gospel displays a special interest in issues of wealth and poverty. There are several warnings against the peril of riches, as in today's Gospel reading (see also Luke 1:53, 6:24f, 16:19–31, for example), and several places where voluntary poverty is commended (12:33; 18:24f; 19:8, for example), or where the gospel message is made specially relevant to the poor (1:52f; 2:8ff; 4:18; 6:20f). Today's passage has much to say to a materialistic age like ours, and sets a particular challenge before the Church: how may society around us see that we live by a different set of values, and not by the materialistic creed of our culture?

Luke's answer to this is very clear: those who truly believe that life does not consist in the abundance of possessions will express that faith by giving: 'Sell your possessions and give alms. Make purses for yourselves that do not wear out, an unfailing treasure in heaven . . . . For where your treasure is, there your heart will be also' (12:33f). In a world of desperate need, our freedom from all kinds of greed (verse 15) will be signalled by our readiness to part with our possessions for the sake of others.

This is the cutting edge of Christian discipleship. Today's readings gather around this theme and show us the roots of this attitude towards possessions.

First, the uselessness of wealth is the theme of the Ecclesiastes reading. The author has experienced all that money can buy (see also 2:8–11), and ends up calling it all vanity of vanities, because (a) it brings no true gain, (b) it causes much hard work, and (c) it must all be left behind. We need to share his down-to-earth perspective. Our reading should really include the last verses of chapter 2, where the author gives a positive response to the despair (2:20) he has just expressed: seeking joy is what life is all about, and God alone is the giver of true joy, to all who please him and seek wisdom.

Second, our accountability to God is the focus of the Gospel passage. 'This very night your soul is required of you!' There is someone – God – who has the right to require our souls, because ultimately we belong to him. Later in the passage Jesus expresses God's expectations, 'From everyone to whom much has been given, much will be required; and from the one to whom much has been entrusted, even more will be demanded' (12:48). We must render account to God for the way we have used resources which are ultimately his.

Third, our life elsewhere is the message of Colossians 3. The basis of the passage is 'You have died, and your life is hidden with Christ in God' (verse 3). We do not belong any more to this world, so we must live by our union with Christ, renouncing all kinds of wrong desire (verse 5), and all forms of wrong speech (verse 8), because our minds are set on 'things above', not on earthly things (verse 2).

These are the theological roots of a radical Christian attitude towards possessions. Our response demands careful thought and prayer.

Theology

In Hosea 11 the metaphor changes from that of the relationship between husband and wife to that of the relationship between father and son. It is a passage of some power and intensity for which there is no parallel in the Old Testament. It recalls the story of Joseph from the patriarchal narratives in Genesis. It also anticipates the parable of the Prodigal Son (Luke 15). It is out of God's overwhelming love for his people that salvation comes. Only the self-giving of parent for child offers so much as an inkling of what this love is like. 'Thou hast made us for thyself, and our heart has no rest till it rests in Thee' (St Augustine).

Ordinary Time – Proper 14

Sunday between 7 and 13 August

Isaiah 1:1,10–20 *with* Psalm 50:1–8,22–23; *or* Genesis 15:1–6 *with* Psalm 33:12–22; Hebrews 11:1–3,8–16; Luke 12:32–40

Believing in the 'second coming' of Christ is something of a minority sport in today's Church. Various sects seem to have hijacked the belief and tainted it with fanaticism. And yet it is a venerable and vital expectation. Venerable, because it has always been part of Church doctrine; and vital, because the shape of biblical faith is essentially future-oriented. This future-orientation is the theme around which today's readings gather.

'I am your shield; your reward shall be very great,' the Lord says to Abraham (Genesis 15:1). For the author to the Hebrews, Abraham shows us what faith is all about, as he launches out in obedience to the promise of God, not seeing its fulfilment except with the eyes of faith. His nomadic lifestyle was only temporary, because God had promised him a dynasty and a home – a city – says Hebrews. Abraham never received it, because the reward is actually heavenly (Hebrews 11:16). So for his whole life he and his family were strangers and foreigners on the earth (verse 13), not at home because their home was elsewhere.

We are in the same position, says the author to the Hebrews. 'Faith is the assurance of things hoped for' (verse 1). That is, the essence of faith is basing action now on the conviction of a state of affairs yet to be. Faith is not just a state of mind, but involves a set of convictions about the destiny of the world, parallel to our convictions about the origin of the world. If we believe that the world has been created, then we may exercise the same faith and believe that it will one day be bettered by its Creator.

Psalm 33 expresses this faith. 'By the word of the Lord the heavens were made, and all their host by the breath of his mouth' (verse 6), and so, 'Our soul waits for the Lord; he is our help and shield . . . . Let your steadfast love . . . be upon us, even as we hope in you' (verses 20,22). Hope arises here out of convictions about origins.

In the New Testament, of course, this faith is focused upon Christ. The Gospel reading expresses it vividly. We do not know when the

Son of Man may come, and so we must live like servants who are always ready for their master's arrival. This does not mean just a passive waiting, however; verses 32–34 describe the constant scurrying around of a Church with this future-oriented faith.

The 'reward' is not something to be sought for itself, but the joyful by-product of a faith directed at Christ himself. The servants focus all their energy and anticipation on the master's return, only to be invited to sit at his table when he comes. We can leave in the realm of speculation the actual mechanics of the coming of the Son of Man and the bettering of the world, but this future-orientation is fundamental to Christian faith, and we dilute it at great cost.

Theology

This week marks the beginning of a series of readings from the 'Letter' to the Hebrews. Modern commentators recognize it as a well-structured sermon or lecture. It seems to have been written to Christians of Jewish origin who were mourning the loss of Jerusalem in 70CE and this raises all sorts of theological questions for the author, not least how on earth to read the scriptures. He clearly regards Jesus as God's Word before whom all revelation is relative, but this was long before Christianity and Judaism went their separate ways – and Christian triumphalism is probably not an appropriate response. By describing the work of Christ as being 'after the order of Melchizedek' – a wholly unique priestly category – the author of Hebrews seems to be affirming that for Christians the Levitical order is no longer operative. All the language of priesthood and victimhood is metaphorical . . . and Christians who try to build penal 'theories' of the atonement on the basis of Hebrews misread the text. It is a homily, in language strange to our ears, which recalls us to the metaphorical nature of all language about God.

Ordinary Time – Proper 15

Sunday between 14 and 20 August

Isaiah 5:1–7 *with* Psalm 80:1–2,8–19; *or* Jeremiah 23:23–29 *with* Psalm 82; Hebrews 11:29–12:2; Luke 12:49–56

Today's Gospel reading contains some puzzles. What 'fire' has Jesus come to bring (verse 49)? What is the 'baptism' which he is eager to fulfil (verse 50)? Do these two pictures refer to the same thing? And how are they related to the following description of division in response to Jesus' ministry?

The reading from Jeremiah 23 suggests what 'fire' may mean, for it uses this image to refer to the word of God spoken in opposition to the misleading words of the false prophets. So perhaps the 'fire' Jesus brings is his prophetic message. But what then would be the kindling for which he longs? Alternatively, 'fire' is a symbol of the Holy Spirit, and Jesus could be looking forward with longing to the gift of the Spirit at Pentecost. But this would not fit well with the surrounding verses, especially the following words about division and conflict. Fire is also (not surprisingly) a regular symbol just for disaster of various kinds (see, for example, Revelation 8:5ff), and maybe that is the simplest explanation of its meaning here.

But why should Jesus bring disaster on the earth? It depends on what sort of disaster is in mind. The picture of family conflict in verses 52–53 is drawn from Micah 7:5–6, where it expresses the alienation experienced by those who want to trust God in the midst of a society which has turned its back on him. Jesus tells his disciples that following him has a similar price tag attached. The life of the servants who wait and work for their master to return will not be easy. In broader terms the author to the Hebrews develops this thought as he describes the faithfulness under fire of those who lived by faith in days past – as an example to us, who must also 'run with perseverance the race that is set before us'.

It has been a constant Jewish objection to Christian faith that Jesus announced the Kingdom, but the world was not redeemed. But we can see from a passage like this that Jesus apparently did not expect the world to be transformed by his ministry – far from it. A sense of the certain coming of final judgment runs through Luke chapter 12, but until that judgment arrives, the earth will be afflicted with division symbolized by the persecution of his followers. In the puzzling verse 56, Jesus is probably referring to his own presence and ministry as a sign of that impending judgment. Like a cloud that heralds a storm, so he points to the final judgment for which all need to prepare.

He does not stand aloof from his suffering Church. In all likelihood, the baptism in verse 50 is his coming death. He, too, was torn by the brokenness and hostility which afflicts our human race and indeed he longs to fulfil that role. What suffering lies ahead of us, as we follow him? Hebrews encourages us with the example of those who were carried through their pain by the vision of the one 'who, for the joy set before him, endured the cross, disregarding its shame, and has taken his seat at the right hand of the throne of God'.

Text

'And what more should I say?' The reading from Hebrews offers a familiar rhetorical device, reminding us that this may well have started out as an oral text. The author's list of precursors of faith stretches from Abel to heroes of the Maccabean revolt (2 Maccabees 6–7), and culminates in Jesus himself, 'the pioneer and perfector' (Hebrews 12:2). Like the faithful generations of the past, Hebrews' present audience also has to look to the future for any final attainment: 'For here we have no lasting city but we seek a city which is to come' (Hebrews 13:14). The promises made to their predecessors were not made good until Jesus' death and enthronement in heaven, so the present audience are exhorted to patience and perseverance. It is Psalm 110 – a royal enthronement psalm – which is influential on the author of Hebrews as on other New Testament writers. He refers to it five times, though only once is it by direct citation (1:13). In this final allusion (12:2) he moves from the aorist to the perfect tense, suggesting that being seated marks the completion of Jesus' work.

Ordinary Time – Proper 16

Sunday between 21 and 27 August

Jeremiah 1:4–10 *with* Psalm 71:1–6; *or* Isaiah 58:9b-14 *with* Psalm 103:1–8; Hebrews 12:18–29; Luke 13:10–17

We often speak of our choice of God. The Bible more often speaks of God's choice of human beings; and a change of emphasis in our testimonies might provide greater insight into the workings of God in the human soul than any number of human claims to have 'chosen' to become a Christian.

Jeremiah clearly did not want to be the prophet that God wanted him to be. And we can hardly blame him. From the account in the book that bears his name, his ministry was not popular: he had to suffer rejection and ridicule, and his message was so unpopular that he was thrown into prison at one stage. Small wonder, then, that he objected, 'Ah, Lord God! Truly I do not know how to speak, for I am only a boy.' Any excuse would seem sensible to avoid such an appalling vocation. Jeremiah might well pray, with the psalmist, for

Background 1

The editors of the book of Jeremiah present the period of Jeremiah's activity as 627–587 (a conventional 'forty-year' motif). Jeremiah may be considered as in some sense continuing Josiah's reformation, but there is nothing in the text which links him specifically to Josiah's time – or indeed to Jehoiakim. The timelessness of the oracles (especially in chapters 2–20) allows them to be used in very different circumstances from those envisaged originally. The association of the speaker named in the title with the reigns of specific kings is also conventional and reflects the presentation of prophecy and monarchy as twin institutions in the history of Israel. Jeremiah the prophet – if he existed – is best dated to the reign of Zedekiah 597–587, but the many knotty complexities of the book need not detract from the timeless messages of its oracles.

refuge from such a life: 'In you, O Lord, I take refuge; let me never be put to shame. In your righteousness deliver me and rescue me; incline your ear to me and save me' – save me from the calling you have given to me!

Jeremiah prophesied in Jerusalem at the time of the city's conquest in 587BCE. He went to Egypt with some of those who were not taken captive to Babylon. He therefore lived in the context of great national upheaval, and part of his message was to insist that what was happening to God's city was the result of God's judgment. So Jeremiah's knowledge of God was not very different from that of the writer of the Epistle to the Hebrews, who wrote that God 'is a consuming fire'. He had no alternative but to hear and obey, for this God is not one to be argued with.

Strangely enough, however, it is precisely this fearsome God of Jeremiah who is the one who brings wholeness to broken lives. The Gospel story reminds us that God is against that which enslaves, and he is for that which heals those who are bowed low with pain and grief. He is against those who say that all is well when it is not; he is against those who use power, not to alleviate anguish, but to exploit their good fortune and ignore the cries of those who suffer. The 'entire crowd' cheered him on – Luke tends to portray Jesus as

Background 2

The Isaiah 58 reading is intended to make sabbath connections with the passage in Luke 13. It gives a vivid picture of the need to focus on sabbath observance in the period after the return from exile. The sabbath has ceased to be understood as a day of rest (verse 13), hard-pressed businesses were functioning and it was no longer central to national life. There is clearly a message here for present-day Christians. The sabbath is more fully recognized among Jews in Britain than Sunday is observed as a day of rest by Christians. The Jewish work ethic is demanding, but the claims of the sabbath are absolute over the religious Jew – in a way that is seldom true for Christians. 'God said to Moses, "I have a precious gift in my treasure house, 'Sabbath' is its name. Go and tell the people of Israel that I wish to give it to them"' (Talmud).

popular with ordinary people; there is no crowd to condemn him at the end, only the religious leaders. So we note and give thanks for the single-mindedness of Jesus in his compassion and his action, since his love never changes. And we stick with the vocation to follow him; where else can we go, since he alone has the words of life?

Ordinary Time – Proper 17

Sunday between 28 August and 3 September

Jeremiah 2:4–13 *with* Psalm 81:1,10–16; *or* Ecclesiasticus 10:12–18 *or* Proverbs 25:6–7 *with* Psalm 112; Hebrews 13:1–8,15–16; Luke 14:1,7–14

Jeremiah's complaint against the people of Judah is that they have abandoned their God, only to put in his place nothing of significance. The oracle he speaks has the tone of a forsaken lover who is bewildered at the folly of the one who has left love and security in exchange for uncertainty, fear and disappointment. The prophet reckons that the generation of Israelites who were led out of Egypt through the wilderness were not so foolish, for when they received the Law through Moses at Sinai they were glad to be in covenant relationship with God. Now the folly of the present generation has cut them off from his promises and his presence, and all they can hope for is desolation and defeat. The psalmist takes up the theme of the people's faithlessness: 'O that my people would listen to me . . ., then I would quickly subdue their enemies . . . . I would feed you with the finest of the wheat, and with honey from the rock I would satisfy you' (81:13–16). Their faithless behaviour is inexplicable, since it will surely end in disaster.

The other readings are also concerned, in their way, with rational behaviour. Why should we act morally? Because of the promise of some repayment, or because 'virtue is its own reward'? In the case of the Letter to the Hebrews, reasons are given for the kind of behaviour recommended – the reference to 'entertaining angels unawares' may be an allusion to Abraham and Sarah's hospitality to the travellers in Genesis 18; three messengers from God visited them to tell them Sarah would have a son the following year. There are also stories in Greek mythology of gods visiting humans 'unawares' and rewarding them for their hospitality. Baucis and Philemon, for example, welcomed Zeus, the king of the gods. When invited to name what their reward should be, they asked that neither should have to mourn the other in their old age. When the day came for them to die, they simultaneously changed into oak trees, remaining on either side of the doorway of their house after they had bidden each other farewell.

The Gospel's exhortation to humility and generosity is made on the basis of the rewards which will be available in the Kingdom of God. Here the issue becomes rather more than a simple discussion of motivation. The Kingdom of God confronts all its hearers with the question of right behaviour for the sake of the behaviour itself. For Christian people the discussion enters a different plane of discourse: to believe that God rewards those who obey him is not the same as believing that we keep an eye on what best serves our interests, first because in Jesus Christ God calls us to live in such a way that the interests of our neighbour are served rather than our own, and second because God is not just one more reward alongside others.

God holds out for us a set of values that are not located in a superficial kind of contract, in which we 'get what we pay for'. The reward of good behaviour for those who seek the mind of God is the knowledge that God delights in love and compassion, and that to behave in such a way is to imitate him whose life and grace we are called to share. This is behaviour that is rooted in an understanding of life in the Spirit.

Application

* Commitments: what keeps our relationships in good repair?
* How do we ensure that our motives are pure, and that we practise good behaviour for its own sake?

Ordinary Time – Proper 18

Sunday between 4 and 10 September

Jeremiah 18:1–11 *with* Psalm 139:1–6,13–18; *or* Deuteronomy
30:15–20 *with* Psalm 1; Philemon 1–21; Luke 14:25–33

Have you ever visited a pottery? Have you watched as the clay is
thrown on to the wheel, and then, with a little water to keep it
moist, is moulded and pushed and pulled until it is fashioned into a
pot? The story of Jeremiah continues with this arresting metaphor of
the potter's wheel. God is portrayed in it as one who creates as a
potter creates a vessel and who brings things to nothing just as the
potter is able to reduce a jar-in-the-making to a shapeless lump
again. This is a chilling picture of God for us who live in an age when
we are aware of the importance of political choices in the world of
international affairs. Aren't our freedoms curtailed by such a reading
of the purposes of God?

And what about Psalm 139? Isn't it quite alarming to think of
someone who knows 'when I sit down and when I rise up', who
'discerns my thoughts from far away' (verse 2)? And do we want to
have someone around to whom it can be said, 'Even before a word is
on my tongue, O Lord, you know it completely' (verse 4). Indeed,
such an image might well 'hem me in, behind and before' (verse 5), in
a sense much more oppressive than the psalmist intends. 'Where is
our freedom?' we may want to ask.

The answer is that it is guaranteed when God is known as the
Father of Jesus Christ, because, in Christ, humanity is called to share
in the life of God. This God is not one who oppresses, but who
generates creativity and who loves the kind of intimacy which makes
for growth and the development of all human potential.

Such a God is set over against any kind of devotion which dimin-
ishes the image of God in us all. That is why the choices are so stark
which confront the people of Israel in Deuteronomy. They have
witnessed God's presence and provision over the years. Will they
now acknowledge his claim to be their God for ever, or will they go
after that which is less than God? Will they choose right or wrong,
life or death? These choices may seem oversimplified – certainly it is
not always easy to discern in the choices we have to make which is

the way of life. But the choice set before the Israelites in this story is one of fundamental attitudes, perceptions and direction; which way do you want your life to go? Answering this question is sometimes easier than living up to its implications.

The choice St Paul set before Philemon was simply concerned with a small favour. Onesimus, a slave whose name means 'useful', had evidently run away from Philemon's household and somehow or other come into contact with the apostle, who had found him very 'useful' to himself. Having made use of his services, Paul sends him back to Philemon, certainly with the intention that Onesimus should not be punished for running away. It is possible that the hidden message, the broad hint, is that Paul wants him sent back to him as a gift, so that he can continue his 'useful' service. We do not know what Philemon decided. Later in the first century there was a bishop of Ephesus called Onesimus. It is comforting to think that this was the former slave, given his freedom, who rose to lead that Christian community not so far away from Colossae. But we do not know.

What we do know is that the choices we make, no matter how small the issue, are all, without exception, the stuff of the Kingdom of God.

Application

* In what ways do people think of God? Is he determined to catch us out, or to bring us to fulfilment? Does he dispose of people and nations by a whim, as a potter does with the clay? What are the signs of his concern for justice for all nations?

Ordinary Time – Proper 19

Sunday between 11 and 17 September

Jeremiah 4:11–12,22–28 *with* Psalm 14; *or* Exodus 32:7–14 *with* Psalm 51:1–10; 1 Timothy 1:12–17; Luke 15:1–10

The prophecy of Jeremiah is concerned here with the judgment that is to come upon the inhabitants of Jerusalem for their apostasy. 'A hot wind' will scorch the earth and all that is in it – and we need to remember that 'wind' is the same word in Hebrew as 'Spirit'. This is God coming in judgment upon his people. The reason for their condemnation was that they had behaved as if God were not to be reckoned with – like the fools in Psalm 14 who had said that there is no God. The psalmist continues, 'They are corrupt, they do abominable deeds; there is no one who does good.' The evil deeds of the people of Judah stemmed from their forgetting their covenant with God.

This is not the same as saying that absence of belief in God necessarily leads to immoral behaviour – we probably all know of atheists who are deeply moral, and we know that the profession of Christian faith is no guarantee that we shall act morally; indeed, we are aware of moral philosophers who say that Christian morality is insufficiently good. However, for the psalmist, the issue was more clear-cut; those who did wrong denied God. Hence the cry, 'O that deliverance for Israel would come from Zion! When the Lord restores the fortunes of his people, Jacob will rejoice; Israel will be glad.' Here is a cry borne of the experience of absence from God, of exile from him.

The 'Pastoral Epistles' – those to Timothy and Titus – are now generally reckoned to have been written by someone other than Paul himself. Their author wrote in Paul's name in order to carry on the tradition of his preaching and teaching, to honour his memory and to continue his ministry. This is not a question of falsehood or trickery, but of loyalty to a tradition. The writer celebrates Paul's memory: his calling is remembered, and he is depicted as the archetypal apostle, changed from blasphemer and persecutor to devoted follower and proclaimer of the good news of Jesus. The grace of God shown to Paul is the subject also of the Gospel reading, where we see that the repentance of the individual person is a matter of concern to God. The Greek word for repentance means a change of mind, and that involves adjusting our mental set to the values of the Kingdom of God.

Moses might provide an example of that. On Mount Sinai he enjoyed the closest possible relationship with God, and was given the Ten Commandments. Yet even while he was there, the people of Israel were deserting the God who had led them out of slavery in Egypt and were constructing a golden calf to worship. Moses, the man of God who was passionately concerned for the good of the people, prayed to God on their behalf and persuaded him not to destroy the people, even though God was offering to make a great nation from Moses' descendants only. However, here was a man who knew God, and who was prepared to forfeit his own spiritual well-being for the sake of those committed to his charge. We often hear of the exploits of those who are prepared to give their lives for the sake of others; how many of us are prepared to sacrifice our salvation?

Application

* In what different ways may faith issue in moral behaviour? The history of the twentieth century provides us with the example of Dietrich Bonhoeffer, who decided that his Christian discipleship must mean plotting to overthrow the tyrannical and murderous Adolf Hitler for the sake of righteousness and for the future of the German nation. Our moral dilemmas rarely reach this pitch, but we do well to think of the difficulty of the decisions faced by those who live in circumstances of extreme political oppression and racial injustice.

Ordinary Time – Proper 20

Sunday between 18 and 24 September

Jeremiah 8:18–9:1 *with* Psalm 79:1–9; *or* Amos 8:4–7 *with* Psalm 113; 1 Timothy 2:1–7; Luke 16:1–13

> There is a balm in Gilead, / To make the wounded whole;
> There is a balm in Gilead / To heal a sin-sick soul.
> Sometimes I feel discouraged / And think my work's in vain;
> But then the Holy Spirit / Revives my soul again.
> There is a balm in Gilead, / To make the wounded whole;
> There is a balm in Gilead / To heal a sin-sick soul.

Today's passage from the prophecy of Jeremiah has him lamenting the desolation of Jerusalem after it has been laid waste by its enemies. The prophet bewails God's absence and calls for help now that the city has been laid waste: is there really no help; is there no 'balm in Gilead'? (verse 22).

The old spiritual suggested that there was comfort, but for Jeremiah himself there is no balm; the situation is desperate. 'My joy is gone, grief is upon me, my heart is sick,' says the prophet. This is the kind of context in which the psalmist (Psalm 79) might well ask, 'How long, O Lord? Will you be angry for ever? Will your jealous wrath burn like fire?' The psalmist wants God's anger to be shown to the nations who have destroyed the city: 'Pour out your anger on the nations that do not know you, and on the kingdoms that do not call on your name, for they have devoured Jacob and laid waste his habitation.' He writes for an age later than Jeremiah, when the mood of the religious thinkers was that God had punished his people enough, and that the surrounding nations had profited too much from Judah's and Israel's defeat. Now the cry is that they be punished for their pride. But earlier, it was God's own people who deserved judgment.

The contrast of this desire for vengeance with the desire in 1 Timothy for prayer on behalf of rulers is quite marked. For a number of reasons it is unlikely that St Paul himself wrote these 'Pastoral Epistles' that bear his name; what is reflected here is a situation in which the Church, presumably before it has known any great persecution on the part of the state, is able to believe that political leaders are there 'so that we may lead a quiet and peaceable life in all godliness and dignity'. A peaceable political state could provide the context in which the gospel could be preached. There are dangers in this view, of course, for the preaching of the gospel may result in conflict with the state's values, as the early Church was soon to discover.

The 'manager' in the Gospel passage can stand for leaders in any context who do not act in charity and compassion towards those who are set under them. Forgiveness, as an instrument of policy, has been shown in many cases to be an effective way of building community and enabling people and groups to function – but it must be exercised equitably; the problem is, all too often, that those at the top of the pile expect to be forgiven, only so that they may exploit their position over their juniors. If we were to read this parable as an allegory (as, it must be admitted, many commentators have done) then we might observe that God is the one who forgives unconditionally, and expects those who are forgiven also, in their turn, to forgive. The allegorical interpretation does not alter the practical, ethical message; it simply gives it both more force and a theological grounding.

Interpretation

* *Has the idea of God's judgment any place in a contemporary understanding of the good news of Jesus Christ? If so, what should that place be? If not, how significant are the moral judgments which we make?*
* *In what ways might the preaching of the gospel in our day bring us into conflict with those who exercise political power?*

Ordinary Time – Proper 21

Sunday between 25 September and 1 October

Jeremiah 32:1–3a,6–15 *with* Psalm 91:1–6,14–16; *or*
Amos 6:1a,4–7 *with* Psalm 146; 1 Timothy 6:6–19; Luke 16:19–31

At the very moment of imminent defeat, Jeremiah tells king Zedekiah of God's purpose to restore the future fortunes of Judah. He tells of his purchase of a field which he or his descendants will claim, once the nation has been brought back from exile in Egypt. The story is told as a reminder of the faithfulness of God. He may have given the city of Jerusalem over to foreign invaders as a punishment for Judah's departure from the covenant, but he will act again in mercy and grace. There may be no hope for the present, but the future is in the hand of God. It is this kind of protection which the psalmist (Psalm 91) can celebrate, not that God will preserve his people from the implications and consequences of their actions, but that they may be certain of his continuing compassion and care for them in the unknown future. 'Those who love me, I will deliver; I will protect those who know my name. When they call to me, I will answer them; I will be with them in trouble, I will rescue them and honour them.'

Amos is railing against the evils of God's people, who constantly refuse to listen to his warnings. They lounge around in luxury and refuse to act in justice towards the poor. Psalm 146 echoes the refrain, 'Do not put your trust in princes, in mortals, in whom there is no help.'

It might not prove as simple for us as the scriptures seem to say that it was for Jeremiah and his contemporaries. Our trust in God has normally to be expressed in and through the relationships we have with other people, and those who claim to have a hotline to the will of the Almighty are rightly regarded with suspicion. However, the principle remains the same. In a context where knowledge of the mind of God was a matter of consulting prophets, what counted was the people's obedience to what was disclosed. For us, although our ways of knowing God are rooted in the conviction that God is known in the everyday jostle of human relationships and concerns, what counts is our commitment to doing the will of God, as we discern what it might be. As the writer of 1 Timothy says, 'There is great gain in godliness combined with contentment.'

This principle is to be applied to the ever-present problem of wealth. (Note: it is wealth, not poverty, that is the problem.) What values are appropriate to the person – or the community – which has more than it can manage or know what to do with? We see in the parable of the rich man and Lazarus the complete folly of a lifestyle and set of values that are dictated by the demands of caring for our earthly possessions. It is not so much that the relationships will be reversed in the life to come; it is that the assumption that wealth is a sign of ultimate well-being is already sufficient proof of folly. Certainly, it is good to have enough money to live on, but a society that condemns so many to live in poverty is foolish, as well as mean and spiritually bankrupt. The values of the Kingdom of God demand more equal sharing of the good things of the world. The values which God proposes for human society are applicable immediately.

Application

* What lessons are there here for the wealth of nations in the world, when many peoples and cultures are left in poverty?
* How do we discern the will of God for our nation, for the Church, for ourselves?

Ordinary Time – Proper 22

Sunday between 2 and 8 October

Lamentations 1:1–6 *with* Lamentations 3:19–26 *or* Psalm 137; *or* Habakkuk 1:1–4; 2:1–4 *with* Psalm 37:1–9; 2 Timothy 1:1–14; Luke 17:5–10

The Book of Lamentations is traditionally ascribed to Jeremiah, but we cannot be certain that he was the author. Although the tenor of the book places it at some point after the destruction of Jerusalem in 587BCE, there are those who think it is later than the time of Jeremiah himself. Nevertheless, it could have been written in the twentieth century. Its bleak description of the city of Jerusalem after it was sacked by the Babylonians reads like something from a battlefield in Flanders or a modern bombed city. Jerusalem has been denuded of its people; all the brightness of city life is no more and there is nothing left, either of its commerce or of its fun. These are the effects of war fought and lost. Yet the writer is still confident of God's compassion; his mercies are 'new every morning'. We may wonder, 'How can you be so sure? What is the evidence? Isn't this no more than "whistling in the dark"?'

In a similar way, the well-known lament in Psalm 137 for the bereft city expresses the psalmist's sorrow at the sacking of Jerusalem. The writer pledges eternal fidelity to the memory of Jerusalem, even though its glory is now departed. How can the vicious sentiments in the final verse have a place in holy scripture? Because holy scripture contains, not just the word of God addressed to humanity, but also the archetypal word which humanity addresses to God; one can imagine this curse on the lips of someone who saw such things happen to the little children of Jerusalem. However, such an explanation of their background can hardly justify their being sung in Christian worship.

The prophet Habakkuk sets a slightly different tone – though not greatly so. Why is it that there is such evil, and why do the just have to suffer so? How terrible it is when 'the law becomes slack and justice never prevails'! Yet the prophets remain true to their calling. They write what they are called to write and speak what they are called to speak. The message is that those who are righteous will gain life by continuing to live in faithfulness to God. This text (Habakkuk 2:4) is the one made famous by St Paul's use of it to mean 'the one who by faith is righteous shall live'; here, in its original context, it calls for fidelity to the covenant, and patience for the working of God. The message of Psalm 37 is similar: do not 'fret' over evildoers; their end will come, and virtue is its own reward.

The two sections of the Gospel passage seem to be connected only by the catchword principle which focuses on the concept of obedience. To the person with faith, trees are obedient when told to plant themselves in the sea. This idea moves on to a consideration of the obedience that is required in servants. When the slave comes in from the field, his work is not done until he has finished serving his owner's desires.

It is possible that there is no connection intended between the opening statement and the continuing story. If they are to be taken together, then whatever the origin of these sayings in the tradition before they were written down, their juxtaposition here suggests that everything is at the disposal of those who have faith; they are privileged to exercise lordship over creation and they may expect obedience. Such is the reversal of the world's values that is to take place at the end of time, when the Kingdom of God dawns.

Interpretation

* *Given the extreme horrors which human history has witnessed in the twentieth century, what place is there for belief in vindication by God of the evil that many people must suffer?*
* *The Bible frequently asserts that faith in God yields the rewards of eventual deliverance and salvation. In the light of our knowledge of other faiths and philosophies in the modern world, is it possible for such a belief to be sustained?*

Ordinary Time – Proper 23

Sunday between 9 and 15 October

Jeremiah 29:1,4–7 *with* Psalm 66:1–12; *or* 2 Kings 5:1–3,7–15c *with* Psalm 111; 2 Timothy 2:8–15; Luke 17:11–19

Now in captivity, the people are advised by Jeremiah to reckon to stay there. They are to settle, to marry and to buy land; indeed they are to reckon with the fact that they must live there for the foreseeable future. Above all, they are to seek the well-being of the place to which they have been taken, for in its prosperity lies their own. The Psalm associated with this reading suggests praise to God for all his decisions about what happens to people; in the context of the Jeremiah passage, it suggests that, whatever happens, whether in the details or in the momentous events of life, God remains God, worthy to be praised for his judgments, which will turn out to be gracious, and his action, which puts his judgments into effect.

The story of Naaman the leper is well known as an incident in the life of the prophet Elisha. Of the points to be noted one might mention the fame of the prophet, the pride of the Syrian commander, the anxiety of the king, the good sense of the serving maid, the willingness of Naaman to swallow his pride – and any number of other details. Clearly, however, what appears to be most important, is the discovery on the part of a non-Jew that 'there is no God in all the earth except in Israel'. Psalm 111 is an appropriate ascription of praise to God for his universal glory and care.

The Second Epistle to Timothy pictures Paul as the great preacher of the gospel, suffering for his faithfulness, yet undiminished in his enthusiasm. The writer (probably not Paul himself) reasserts the gospel as he understands it, and urges that the tradition of teaching must continue which started with the apostle. The emphasis on 'rightly explaining' is significant: it suggests the careful cutting of 'sections' of the truth, to enable people to take in what they need. A sensitive approach to other people's learning is what is required.

The Gospel passage makes a connection with the story of Naaman, the Syrian. It shows, first, the unity of those in need: no distinctions of race are made between the lepers who all need cleansing. Neither does Jesus discriminate. What strikes him, though, is the

148

significant fact that it was the 'outsider' who alone returned to express his thanks. This has implications for Luke's understanding of the gospel; in the Acts of the Apostles this emphasis on its appeal to those outside the traditional people of God will become apparent. There are parallels for us, in a society in which many wish to place barriers between people and make exclusions where God invites all people to know and be known by him.

Interpretation

Naaman was an 'outsider', not being a member of the Jewish race, yet this story shows Judaism as able to live with an acknowledgement of its God without any insistence on conversion. Is it possible that an insistence on the importance of conversion might constitute an inappropriate barrier between people? In a society as diverse in terms of religion and ethnicity as our own, how might barriers between religions be broken down?

Ordinary Time – Proper 24

Sunday between 16 and 22 October

Jeremiah 31:27–34 *with* Psalm 119:97–104; *or* Genesis 32:22–31 *with* Psalm 121; 2 Timothy 3:14–4:5; Luke 18:1–8

The lesson from Jeremiah is one of the most touching of Old Testament passages. Here the Lord God promises to restore a covenant relationship with the people, but one which is different from what existed prior to the exile which the people are now suffering. Formerly, God tells Jeremiah, the people had to apply themselves to keeping the covenant and knowing God; but when the nation's fortunes are restored, they will have no need of any exhortations to faithfulness, because God will give them his own Spirit, so they will keep his Law without having to struggle to do so.

The modern reader may wince at this prediction of automated obedience, but Christians will see it as a foretaste of life in the Holy Spirit, where what counts as good behaviour is not adherence to any set of standards or rules or law, but the expression of the Spirit of God, who is also the Spirit of the risen Jesus, in the life of the believer. The psalmist celebrates the Law of God because it represents God's favour to Israel; it is thus a symbol of the covenant, as well as the content of it. It may stand as a metaphor, both for Christian adherence to the scriptures, and for the Christian's desire to do the will of God as the Spirit leads.

The lesson from Genesis tells the wonderful story of Jacob receiving his come-uppance at the hands of the angel of the Lord. He may have won the wrestling match, but he lived ever after with the wound received in the fight. His experience is not very different from life in the Spirit. We have no guarantee against harm; indeed, some of our ills arise because of our faith. And sometimes we limp a little, because we are called to 'bear in our body the marks of the Lord Jesus'. Faith is not the passport to a trouble-free existence; it is the awareness that whatever happens to us is shared by a God who loves us and who is with us in all of it.

The writer of 2 Timothy continues to exhort Timothy to exercise leadership in the Christian community by teaching the faith; his pastoral care is not separated from telling the people how to understand the scriptures (in his case, the Jewish scriptures, whether in Hebrew or in Greek) in the light of Christ. Such an attachment to understanding the holy writings of the community is central to discipleship; and any understanding of 'pastoral care' which is held apart from the importance of learning fails to do justice to the nature of either.

Jesus' parable in Luke 8 is not the easiest to understand. Its basic message is relatively simple: there are those who will respond to requests on the basis of impatience and self-interest, but God delights in giving gifts to his people. Christian people therefore should pray without stopping, for to pray is to continue in conversation with God. Jesus' final sentence sounds like a weary sigh, emitted in the awareness that, even though God is so gracious, men and women are inexplicably reluctant to talk and share their lives with him.

Application

What is our experience of intercessory prayer? Do we find our prayers 'answered' – or are we rather ourselves changed by the process and helped to accept the hard facts of life?

Ordinary Time – Proper 25

Sunday between 23 and 29 October

Joel 2:23–32 *with* Psalm 65; *or* Sirach 35:12–17 *or* Jeremiah
14:7–10,19–22 *with* Psalm 84:1–7; 2 Timothy 4:6–8,16–18;
Luke 18:9–14

The prophet Joel looks forward with glad anticipation to the day, not just when the exiles will return to Jerusalem, but when the Lord himself will return, and give his Spirit to the people, so that they will worship him in spirit and be marked out as his people. Then he will vindicate them for all that they have suffered at the hands of other nations. That is the picture that is also drawn in the Psalm which is associated with this reading – of the people of God glad in their knowledge of him and giving thanks for his blessing, not only on themselves, but also on the earth itself.

The Wisdom of Jesus ben Sirach, otherwise known as Ecclesiasticus, is a typical example of Wisdom literature. The title means 'The Community Book'. Here it urges justice in human relationships, for God is no respecter of persons; when it says that he will not show partiality to the poor, it means that the possession or non-possession of wealth is not an issue when it comes to God's justice. What is important is whether the person has acted rightly; and both rich and poor are capable of good and evil. The Jeremiah passage returns again to the same theme of judgment and mercy which the lectionary has covered over the past several weeks. Here the prophet acknowledges the sins of the people before God, and prays for forgiveness. He is confident in God's abiding faithfulness, even if the tragedy facing Jerusalem is now unavoidable. Psalm 84 seems all the more poignant in such a context. The dwelling place of God is the temple at Jerusalem, and those who once lived in God's house, ever singing his praise, were bereft of such blessings once the place had been desecrated and abandoned.

St Paul's memory is hallowed once again in 2 Timothy. The apostle is shown contemplating his end, reviewing his life and summing up his achievements. The Epistle has no doubt that Paul 'fought the good fight' and 'kept the faith'. He may have been beset by opposition throughout his ministry – and there is a tradition in the First Epistle of Clement that he was betrayed at the end by Christian opponents. But this hero of the faith is held up as the model disciple, whom all other disciples should emulate.

The parable of the Pharisee and the publican brings all the discussion about faith and faithfulness to basics. What is significant is not so much the faithfulness of the disciple, but the faithfulness of God who is dependably gracious. In the sight of God, what is required is not the elaboration of our achievements, but the acknowledgement of our shortcomings. The grace of God is not out to minimize our successes, but it does put into perspective our sometimes vaunted accomplishments. Paul himself knew (compare Philippians 3) that everything he had done, for good or ill, counted for nothing when set beside the infinite mercy of God. Today's readings invite us to a similar reflection upon the mercy we have all received.

Application

How can looking back to re-count God's blessings avoid the danger of nostalgia?

Bible Sunday

Isaiah 45:22–25; Psalm 119:129–136; Romans 15:1–6;
Luke 4:16–24

'Bible Sunday' presents an opportunity to celebrate the presence of the holy scriptures, not just in the life of the Church, but also in and among all humankind. Historically, it is certainly the Church within which the scriptures arose, but there is no doubt that their message is one for the whole of humankind, for they speak of God who became human in the person of Jesus.

The passage from Isaiah reminds us that the 'word' of God cannot easily be identified with a written text, for it existed and was active before anything was written. For Isaiah, that which God speaks is that which brings things into being, and it cannot fail to achieve what God wants it to create. 'From my mouth has gone forth in righteousness a word that shall not return' is indicative of Isaiah's understanding of the word of God, which calls all people to worship the one God, made known in Israel's history, and, for Christian people, known as the Father of Jesus Christ.

The Psalm reflects the wonder of the written Torah, or Law, of the Jewish nation as it is revered still. The Law is a sign of the covenant, and it is given to the Jewish nation as a mark of God's choice. In singing the praises of the Law, the psalmist is also praising God for revealing it to the human race through the Jews. It is into this same inheritance that Christians enter, by the grace of God. St Paul catches the flavour of this when he writes to the Romans, 'For whatever was written in former days was written for our instruction, so that by steadfastness and by the encouragement of the scriptures we might have hope.' He refers, of course, to the Jewish scriptures, which formed the first Bible for the early Christians; the 'New Testament' as we know it, was not finalized until later in Christian history.

From the very start, Christians have read the Jewish scriptures as though they speak of Christ. In a sense, of course, they do, though perhaps not in ways which Christians originally thought. Over the past two centuries, Christian scholars have come to recognize a little of the processes that went into the formation of the Christian Bible; it has become obvious that the primary meaning of Jewish scriptures is not simply as prophecy of Christ and the Church, but as integral to the life and faith of the Jewish people. To these were added, first, the letters of St Paul, along with other letters and the Gospels.

The story in Luke 4 is instructive: it shows how the earliest Christians used the text of the Bible to give meaning to their understanding of the significance of Jesus. But more than that, it shows, in a fashion typical of Jewish faith and continued among Christians, that texts are capable of many interpretations. The people who listened to Jesus in that synagogue would not have been surprised that he used the occasion to explore a novel meaning of the text; what they objected to was that he referred the text to himself. We too operate in this double way. The text of scripture has meaning in its context, the 'historical–grammatical sense,' as Martin Luther called it; and from this has developed the biblical critical approach which is used throughout Western Christendom. But it also demands the understanding of faith, and so points to Jesus, as it were, in defiance, not only of Jewish objections, but also of any tradition which would limit the senses in which Jesus can be understood and known today and in any age.

Dedication Festival

First Sunday in October or Last Sunday after Trinity

1 Chronicles 29:6–12; Psalm 122; Ephesians 2:19–22; John 2:13–22

There is a dilemma at the heart of Christianity which persists throughout the scriptures. It concerns the value to be put on things physical – the handiwork both of God and of human beings. To what extent may places, trees and rocks be set apart and regarded as 'holy'? The answers vary along a spectrum. At one end there is superstition about 'things', an inability to move beyond seeing God in the present order (whether that be nature or some religious institution). At the other end is a refusal to see the sacred anywhere specific and to 'spiritualize' faith out of all engagement with the created order, lacking either ecological awareness or political cutting edge. The two poles emerge as equally limited. Both in their different ways short-circuit the essential integration between spirit and matter implied by belief in an incarnate God. Today's readings offer a warning to the contemporary Church as it tries to walk a fine line between thinly spread political activism on the one hand and navel-gazing 'spirituality' on the other. There are innumerable instances where we make a false distinction between our outer and our inner beings.

The Book of Chronicles, from which the first reading comes, endeavours to rethink long-held beliefs and adapt to a lifestyle no longer dependent on a king or on national freedom. Moving away from a traditional stress on prophecy, the small Jewish community under Persian rule is beginning to become a 'religion' and to emphasize the value of temple worship and ritual purity. In a time when alien rule seems likely to go on for ever and when no future messianic age is in view, the chronicler recommends political quietism, submission to destiny and a high view of religious practice – giving hope to Judah. The Lord is always with his people, especially when they are at worship.

The passage from Ephesians offers an interesting hinge between the positive view of religion, presented in the Old Testament reading, and the prophetic action of Jesus in the Gospel – implying judgment on the Jerusalem Temple. Ephesians emerges from a period, rather like that of Chronicles, in which the religious task is that of accom-

156

modating theology to political reality. The main difference is that there is no longer a sacrificial system or physical building upon which to focus. Instead the author describes God's plan as being worked out on two different levels: the heavenly and the earthly. Here his images for the (earthly) Church will provide the basis for instruction in Christian behaviour. Jews and Gentiles are now members of one household, a building growing into a holy temple; but it is the Spirit, rather than a physical structure, which enables unity and growth. Despite the static imagery, there is some inner dynamism and movement within the secure, and conventional, scenario.

Temple imagery is used in a variety of ways in the New Testament. The Ephesians picture may be a development of Paul's 'Body of Christ' (1 Corinthians 12) taken with the tradition in John's Gospel that Jesus himself likened his own 'body' to the temple. It is this second image which comes to the fore in the Gospel reading. Jesus makes his epiphany, or appearance, at the temple in Jerusalem – and replaces the temple as the place of God's revelation. Unlike the other Gospel accounts this happens at the very beginning of his ministry, and there is misunderstanding, typical of this Gospel, as to what he is really about. The notion of physical and spiritual realities as indivisible is expressed throughout the biblical material – not least in the person of Jesus. It points us towards the possibility of understanding the material world and human creativity – even our Church communities – as graced by God for mission. Where they remain static, as ends in themselves, they fall under judgment.

Application

What criteria might be applied to enable us to understand the nature of holiness as applied (a) to people and (b) to things?

All Saints' Sunday

Daniel 7:1–3,15–18; Psalm 149; Ephesians 1:11–23; Luke 6:20–31

The visions of the Book of Daniel are remarkable creations, in which beasts of all kinds of awesome detail strike terror into the minds of the readers. The Book of Daniel was written to assert and encourage the faith of a community which, in the first part of the second century BCE, was under siege. The great encouragement here was that, in the middle of all this terror, when God's people were suffering atrocious things for their faith, the image of 'one like a man' was set to remind them of the supreme value to God of those people, human beings, who comprised his saints: 'As for these four great beasts, four kings shall arise out of the earth. But the holy ones of the Most High shall receive the kingdom and possess the kingdom for ever and ever.' As the psalmist says (verse 4), 'For the Lord takes pleasure in his people; he adorns the humble with victory.'

God's 'holy ones' are, of course, his saints; the word is the same. But the saints in scripture are not the special people singled out as holier than the rest of their brothers and sisters; they are the whole community, chosen by God to be 'set apart' from the nations of the earth. The writer of the Epistle to the Ephesians – probably a disciple of Paul – knew this well. According to him, the destiny of the people of Israel, who were undoubtedly chosen by God to be his 'holy ones', was now to be the destiny of the whole human race, for in Christ, God had made known his desire that non-Jews were also blessed and brought into covenant relationship with him.

The message of Jesus as it is set out by St Luke makes it more specific. Luke is concerned for the outsider and the outcast; in his version of the gospel story Jesus calls the outcast into a life of friendship with God that knows no boundaries and which brings about a change of life and attitude. The standards of normal human and earthly assumptions are turned around. Where the rich are considered of most value; where the over-satisfaction of appetites is thought to be the highest goal of human striving; where laughter and 'looking on the bright side' are the only homely advice that conventional wisdom can offer; and where the all-important factor in what is worth doing is whether it will look good on your *curriculum vitae* – Jesus comes along and says, 'On the contrary: poverty is a closer

158

indicator of value with God; hunger is preferable to the indulgence that is generally regarded as deserving of worth; to weep and to mourn are surer ways of knowing the presence of God; and persecution and reviling are better than the accolades of a culture whose values are jaded, censorious and exclusive. The only way to live is to love – even your enemies; the only way to find meaning and retain some sense of human worth is to ignore the condemnation of those who would despise you for your simple lifestyle and your refusal to be bludgeoned into following the latest fashion – even when it is a religious one.'

Christians – and other holy people – who have followed this way have never been popular, nor have they ever been easy to live with. But they have pointed to a way of living which most of us aspire to on our best days but shun most of the time; shallowness is so much more comfortable. We give thanks today for those who have had the courage to remind us that there is a better way of living, which does not seem so at the time, but the rewards of which are longer term and infinitely more satisfying.

The Fourth Sunday before Advent

Sunday between 30 October and 5 November

Isaiah 1:10–18; Psalm 32:1–7; 2 Thessalonians 1:1–12;
Luke 19:1–10

In the final weeks of the liturgical year the lectionary offers a series of readings which centre on the theme of 'the Kingdom'. The period from All Saints' Day to Advent brings together the themes of All Saints, All Souls, Remembrance Sunday and, in some traditions, the Kingship of Christ. Thus we affirm Christian things about holy people and about dead people within the context of a belief that Christ is King, as we look forward to Advent, which itself looks forward to the coming of Jesus at Christmas.

With savage irony the prophet Isaiah weighs into the city of Jerusalem, comparing it to the cities of Sodom and Gomorrah in Genesis, whose evil was legendary. There is heavy sarcasm in verse 18. The claims to snowlike purity and woollen softness are to be spoken with the kind of intonation that implies, 'Do you really believe this is to be the case?' To complete the passage, the reader needs to continue to verses 19 and 20: 'If you are willing and obedient, you shall eat the good of the land; but if you refuse and rebel, you shall be devoured by the sword; for the mouth of the Lord has spoken.' This is no cosy promise to forgive and forget!

Having said that, it is clear that penitence and contrition bring forgiveness and restoration. The psalmist knew that; even if his experience of impenitence led him to despair. It is this that lies at the root of biblical condemnations of sin. Those who know the will of God and who fail to observe it are those who stand in greater danger of eternal loss than those who never knew themselves to be numbered among the people of God.

Such is the burden of the message of the opening chapter of 2 Thessalonians. This may have been written by a disciple of Paul in order to 'correct' those who said that the Kingdom of God had already come and therefore to urge a more patient and world-affirming life of holiness. Judgment will come, but in God's good time.

The story of Zacchaeus paints a picture of response to and delight in acceptance and forgiveness. It is worth noting several features of the story: first, the nature of the man – small in stature, limited in perspective and petty in aspiration; second, the initiative of Jesus – it is he who looks up and invites himself to eat with this collaborator, cheat and outsider; third – the point of the story – the whole reason for the coming of Jesus is 'to seek and to save the lost'. And Zacchaeus can almost be seen to grow taller as he is restored again as an upright son of Abraham.

Such is the nature of God's free and unconditional love. In Jesus, he moves out in pity – even for the pitiless – and widens the horizons of the greedy; not so that they will take yet more, but so that they become able to give.

The Third Sunday before Advent

Sunday between 6 and 12 November

Job 19:23–27a; Psalm 17:1–9; 2 Thessalonians 2:1–5,13–17;
Luke 20:27–38

Today's readings are all about disputes: Job with God, the psalmist with his enemies, 2 Thessalonians with those who say that the return of Jesus has already happened, and Jesus with the Sadducees.

The passage from the Book of Job is about vindication. Job insists that there exists somewhere the person who will act as his redeemer, in the technical sense of the person in Jewish law who would come to his side and stand to take responsibility for him – as did Boaz for Ruth in her widowhood. 'In the end of the day,' he says, 'the goodness of my life will be apparent, and I will be clear that I have suffered unjustly.' The theme continues in the Psalm, with the psalmist justly insisting on his righteousness and pleading for God to listen to his pleas and show his love. The writer's enemies are hemming him in, and he needs God to demonstrate the justice of his cause.

The reading from 2 Thessalonians continues with the writer appearing to insist, in the face of those who maintain that the final coming of the Lord has already taken place, that the 'second coming' will not happen until there has been a general period of lawlessness. He thanks God for the faith and faithfulness of the Christians in Thessalonica and reminds them that they are called to 'obtain glory' when the Lord does eventually return. Therefore they are to 'stand firm and hold fast to the traditions that [they] were taught'. Such language suggests that this is someone writing after Paul's time, for he clearly thought that the Lord's coming was imminent, and it seems more likely that one of his followers, rather than the apostle himself, would want to take the disciples back, as it were, to a tradition of teaching, rather than point them forward to the new direction in which the Spirit was leading.

The Gospel passage has Jesus in dispute with the Sadducees, the group who, we are told, denied any belief in the resurrection. Their trick question is about life 'in the resurrection', and Jesus answers them by taking to task the crudity of their expectations. Resurrection life is not a matter of who belongs to whom; it is about life in the spirit, where the knowledge of God makes possible relationships which transcend normal earthly categories.

What are we to make of these conflicts today, when the opponents of the biblical writers seem to have right on their side? Frequently, now, 'crudity' is to be seen on the part of believers! Many would say that we need to interpret a belief in a literal 'second coming' in the light (a) of what we know about the background to such beliefs in the earliest years of the Church's life and (b) of two millennia of Christian history and theology which inevitably have removed any sense of imminence from faith. The future, for Christian people, symbolizes immediacy of the Kingdom of God which is always ahead of us. To insist on its literal coming at some indeterminate point in the future is to deny the daily demands of faith, and to deny the validity of the metaphor is to abandon any grounds for hope in the future.

The Second Sunday before Advent

Sunday between 13 and 19 November

Malachi 4:1–2a; Psalm 98; 2 Thessalonians 3:6–13; Luke 21:5–19

Judgment is the theme of the reading from Malachi, along with a promise of restoration for those who 'revere God's name'. The psalmist sings songs of God's victory and the vindication of his people, hence all creation must sing with him.

The theme of the Lord not returning yet is continued in 2 Thessalonians. 'Idlers' probably think that, since the Lord has returned, they do not need to do anything – even work to earn a living. Paul – or the person writing in Paul's name – reminds them of Paul's conduct among them as a non-stipendiary apostle, who earned his own living while preaching the gospel, so as not to be a financial burden to them, and so as to provide them with an example. The lesson is one against sentimentalism; a vibrant faith in Christ leads, not to indolence and a dreamy assumption that other people will support our religiosity, but to a commitment to life, work and the pursuit of a holiness that is rooted in earthly realities.

The reading from Luke comes at the start of the lengthy speech of Jesus (included in each of the Synoptic Gospels) during the Lord's last days in Jerusalem. Following the story of the widow's mite, the conversation turns to the beauty of the temple, and Jesus predicts its downfall. When asked when this is to happen, he warns his disciples against too hasty an assumption that the coming of God's Kingdom will be subject to any particular individual's claims. All sorts of other things are to happen first.

The consistent theme here is that of living in the world in the light of the world to come, but with no unhealthy obsession with piety or religiosity. Faith is to be rooted in the here and now, and the future, precisely because it is in God's hands, can take care of itself. Such a view stands in stark contrast with those other-worldly approaches to believing which take no account of how life is to be lived, and which set a higher store on thinking the right things and having the right experiences than on living a righteous life.

The whole point of Christian existence in the world is the pursuit of human holiness! Those who 'revere God's name' are those who keep his commandments. Jesus also said, 'Not everyone who says to me, "Lord, Lord," will enter the kingdom of heaven, but only the one who does the will of my Father in heaven.'

Christ the King

Jeremiah 23:1–6; Psalm 46; Colossians 1:11–20; Luke 23:33–43

A number of themes are present on this last Sunday before Advent: the Feast of Christ the King; the implications of the kingdom for all earthly rule; and the traditional 'Sunday next before Advent', or 'Stir up Sunday', in Anglican piety.

'Shepherds' in the Bible frequently stand for kings, the rulers of God's people. So the message is to those who exercise authority over others – in whatever context, not just in the Church; for the effect of Jesus is to make the spiritual tradition of the children of Israel applicable to all nations and people. God promises to take care himself of those whom the politicians forget; he expects rulers to rule with compassion. Hence the psalmist's conviction 'God is our refuge and strength, a very present help in trouble' for those who have no other access to power, influence and control, even over their own lives. The question is: what is the evidence for this? What are such statements worth in the real terms of contemporary discourse?

An answer is provided from the Letter to the Colossians, and it is Christ and the Church. The Church is not set against the world, but is part of it, praying for it, longing for its contemporary and immediate salvation, and trusting that God will soon come and vindicate those who need comfort and advocacy amid the ruthlessness that determines public life which forgets the poor and the excluded. The Church's function is to be human, in imitation of Christ, on behalf and in anticipation of a humanity that still awaits its salvation and wholeness in Christ.

In a sense it is remarkable – though in another sense not so – that all this talk of 'kingdom' brings the reader to Calvary. The kind of divine kingship that is conveyed in the total life of Jesus is one of love and sacrifice. The sacrifice of Jesus is a forgiving act (see verse 34 'Father, forgive'), and the penitent thief stands for all who turn, at whatever end or whatever extremity, to the God who is the Father of Jesus; both the response and the promised healing are immediate in the 'Today . . .' of Jesus' answer.

Such kingship is worlds away from the need to control and the conviction of superiority that usually afflicts leaders. What might it mean for those of us who exercise leadership in the Church, the State, or in any community or group, to follow such a leadership style? We might seek to draw out the best of discipleship and love; we might give up controlling and instead seek ways of setting others free to explore who they are and what they might become, by the grace of God; we might deny ourselves the glory of accolades from other people and delight only in the joy of those we lead and serve.

As we stir our Christmas puddings, we might pray for the Spirit of God to stir up our lives to take seriously the call to love and serve on behalf of him who 'came not to be served, but to serve, and to give his life a ransom for many'.

Table of First Sunday after Trinity dates and Propers

YEAR	SUNDAY CYCLE	FIRST SUNDAY AFTER TRINITY	PROPER
2001	C	17 June	6
2002	A	2 June	4
2003	B	22 June	7
2004	C	13 June	6
2005	A	29 May	4
2006	B	18 June	6
2007	C	10 June	5
2008	A	25 May	(3)*
2009	B	14 June	6
2010	C	6 June	5
2011	A	26 June	8
2012	B	10 June	5
2013	C	2 June	4
2014	A	22 June	7
2015	B	7 June	5
2016	C	29 May	4
2017	A	18 June	6
2018	B	3 June	4
2019	C	23 June	7
2020	A	14 June	6

* For Proper 3 use Second Sunday before Lent, Option B (8th Sunday after Epiphany)

Subject index

Abraham, 103, 123, 124, 125–6, 129, 136
Advent, 1, 3–5, 8, 10, 160, 162, 164, 166
Angels, xi, 13, 21, 26, 27, 55, 90, 95, 136
Anna, 35–6, 37
Ascension, xi, 93, 95–6, 97
Augustine, 128

Baptism, 28–9, 32, 39, 59, 131, 132
Benedictus, 3
Bible, ix-x, 6–7, 12, 14–15, 47, 55, 56, 64, 91, 92, 133, 147, 154–5, 166
Birth, xi, 8, 12, 14, 16, 17, 21, 22, 36, 95

Change, 5, 30, 52, 59, 66, 86, 97, 98, 126, 140, 158
Christmas, 1, 11, 13, 16, 17, 18, 20, 22, 30, 39, 87, 160, 167
Church, ix-x, 2, 3, 9, 25–6, 30–1, 40, 42, 53, 55, 66, 68, 75, 81, 84–5, 87, 90, 91, 96, 97, 103–4, 109, 110, 115, 117, 125, 126, 127, 129, 130, 132, 142–3, 145, 154, 156–7, 166–7
Circumcision, 62, 105
Community, xii, 9, 13, 38, 44, 52, 54, 56, 66, 69, 75, 77, 81, 84, 89, 91, 93, 104, 139, 143, 145, 150, 152, 156, 158, 167
Cornelius, 91, 105–6

Covenant, 11, 56, 60, 62, 80, 103, 136, 140, 144, 147, 150, 154, 158
Creation, 16, 19, 20, 23, 46, 72, 82, 91, 99, 100, 103, 119, 122, 147
Cross, 26, 27, 51, 64, 66, 70–1, 72, 79, 80, 119, 132
Crucifixion, 4, 66, 79, 82, 86, 93, 103
Culture, xi, 2, 26, 52, 68, 86, 92, 98, 127, 159

Damascus, 105, 109, 114
David, 7, 11–12, 14, 61, 78, 81, 104, 111–12
Death, ix, 7, 15, 22, 23, 28, 38, 42, 43, 45–6, 48, 54, 62–3, 66, 69, 70–3, 74, 76–7, 79, 84–5, 91, 95, 103, 104, 110, 114, 132, 138
Deuteronomy, 54
Discipleship, x, 52, 54–5, 57–8, 63, 66, 68, 69, 70, 74, 76, 80, 81, 87, 88, 94, 116, 127, 140–1, 151, 167

Easter, xi, 52, 80, 82, 84–8, 89, 91, 93, 97
Emmaus, xi
Environment, 46
Ephesus, 139
Epiphany, 25, 27, 28, 30, 32, 35, 157
Exile, 11, 22, 71, 77, 80, 82, 134, 140, 144, 150

Faith, ix, 1, 42, 43, 47, 53, 54, 56,
    57, 59, 69, 72, 75, 76, 77, 78, 80,
    81, 86, 89, 90, 91, 92, 93, 97, 98,
    99, 104, 105–6, 108, 112, 114,
    119, 120, 121, 125, 127, 129–30,
    131, 140, 147, 150, 152–3, 155,
    156, 158, 162–3
Faithfulness, 11, 19, 78, 131, 144,
    147, 148, 150, 152, 153, 162
Fear, 13, 28, 47, 79, 90, 136
Flood, 47
Forgiveness, 28, 45, 53, 62, 76,
    111–12, 121, 143, 152, 160,
    161
Freedom, 13, 50, 54, 62, 69, 70, 84,
    116, 127, 138, 139, 156

Gifts, 25, 31, 59, 103, 151
Glory, 4, 18, 28, 39, 50–1, 53, 58,
    68, 72, 73, 74, 82, 86, 91, 92, 94,
    99, 146, 148, 167
God's name, 28
Golden Calf, 141

Hannah, 64
Healing, 34, 41, 49, 62, 66, 107,
    166
Holy Spirit, xi, 16, 28, 29, 31, 68,
    101–2, 103, 105, 107, 126, 131,
    142, 150
Hope, 1, 2, 65, 77, 80, 82, 97, 113,
    114, 120, 121, 129, 136, 144,
    154, 156, 163

Idolatry, 59
Incarnation, 1, 7, 9, 11, 24, 69
Irenaeus, xii

Jacob, 140, 142, 150
Jerusalem, 1, 11, 16, 24, 25, 28,
    30–1, 35, 37, 42, 55, 58, 60, 66,
    68, 70, 75, 79, 82, 91, 93, 99,
    103, 108, 109, 114, 130, 134,
    140, 142, 144, 146, 152, 157,
    160, 164

Jews, 12, 16, 25, 26, 28, 35, 62–3,
    71, 96, 105, 106, 109, 121–2,
    126, 130, 154–5, 156–7, 158
John the Baptist, 3, 5, 18, 28
Joseph of Arimathea, 81
Joseph, husband of Mary, 20–1, 38,
    45
Judaism, 31, 63, 94, 112, 125, 130,
    149
Judgment, 1, 3, 5–6, 52, 74, 79, 80,
    99, 104, 122, 131–2, 134, 140,
    142, 143, 152, 156, 157, 160,
    164
Just, 3, 5, 8, 146
Justice, 2, 5–6, 9, 44, 50, 52, 71,
    90, 111, 139, 144, 146, 151, 152,
    162
Justification, 114

Kingdom, xii, 11, 18, 35, 37, 40,
    41, 46, 71, 77, 82, 95, 96, 98,
    103, 117, 119, 121, 122, 131,
    137, 139, 141, 145, 147, 158,
    160, 163, 166

Lamb, 86, 94, 98
Last Supper, 63, 68, 74–76
Law, 9, 19, 32, 44, 66, 74, 93, 94,
    106, 109, 111, 114–15, 120, 122,
    136, 146, 150, 154, 162
Lazarus, 145
Lent, 39, 47, 49, 51, 52, 53, 54, 57,
    59, 62, 66
Life, ix, xi-xii, 3, 5, 15, 19, 20, 23,
    28, 29, 38, 41, 43, 45, 46, 53, 54,
    59, 64, 67, 68, 70, 77, 79, 82,
    84–5, 86, 89, 91, 92, 95–6, 100,
    102, 104, 110, 113, 117, 126,
    127, 128, 129, 131, 134, 135,
    137, 138–9, 143, 145, 147, 148,
    150, 152, 155, 158, 162, 163,
    164, 166, 167
Light, 1, 13, 18, 37, 44, 50, 51, 70,
    72, 73, 74, 81, 85, 94, 98, 103,
    108, 151, 164

Logos, 101
Lord's Supper, 103–4
Love, xi, 1, 4, 6, 9, 11, 13, 19,
    26, 27, 29, 31, 32, 36, 44, 45, 54,
    63, 65, 74, 77, 79, 85, 86, 87,
    91–2, 97, 99, 102, 104, 111, 119,
    120, 121, 124, 128, 129, 135,
    136, 137, 144, 159, 161, 162,
    167

Magi, 25, 32
Magnificat, 8, 68
Manna, 62
Marcion, xii
Martha 156–7
Martyrdom, 70
Mary, mother of Jesus, 20–1, 35,
    37, 38, 64–5, 70, 71
Mary Magdalene 83
Mary, sister of Martha 156–7
Mercy, 2, 5, 6–7, 80, 91, 144, 152,
    153
Messiah, 9, 11, 28, 33, 37, 71, 112,
    114
Micah, 131
Miracles, 20, 104, 110
Mission, xii, 25, 54, 73, 88, 119,
    157
Moses, 19, 49–51, 58, 93, 108, 109,
    134, 136, 141
Motherhood, 64–5

Nicodemus, 81
Numbers, 29

Obedience, 9, 17, 69, 70, 86, 92,
    104, 108, 122, 129, 144, 147,
    150

Pain, 2, 14, 32, 36, 49, 64, 82, 108,
    113, 125–6, 132, 134
Parable, 60, 121–2, 128, 143, 145,
    151, 153
Patience, 9, 71, 132, 147
Paul, xii, 3, 7, 26–7, 30–1, 36, 39,
    40, 43, 45–6, 49–51, 52, 57, 62,
    65, 69, 72–3, 76, 82, 86, 87, 91,
    94, 97–8, 99, 101, 103, 105–6,
    108–9, 111–12, 114–15, 116,
    119, 121, 122, 125, 139, 140,
    142–3, 148, 152, 154, 158, 160,
    164
Penitence, 59, 78, 80, 160
Pentecost, xi, 95, 97, 99, 103, 131
People of God, xii, 30, 60, 71, 72,
    78, 149, 152, 160
Peter, xii, 39–40, 58, 79, 80, 82–3,
    87, 109, 112
Poor, 8, 33, 34, 38, 41, 113, 123,
    127, 144, 152, 166
Prayer, 9, 18, 28, 47, 52, 54, 57,
    58, 77, 84, 94, 97, 112, 115, 121,
    125–6, 128, 136, 151
Prophecy 6, 8, 14–15 37, 64, 74,
    82, 122, 133–4, 140, 142, 154
Prophets, 1, 5–6, 11, 14–15, 16, 19,
    49, 52, 59, 67, 71, 74, 78, 108–9,
    117, 121, 122, 125, 126, 131,
    133–4, 136, 142, 144, 146, 148,
    152, 160

Redemption, 36, 37, 38, 67, 121
Religion, 1, 2, 52, 53, 72, 76, 106,
    112, 122, 149, 156–7
Repentance, 52, 60, 62, 86, 141
Resurrection, xi, 7, 15, 31, 41,
    42–3, 45–6, 66, 82–3, 84–5, 86,
    88, 89, 91, 93, 95, 96, 101, 131,
    163
Revelation, 19, 25, 41, 47, 48, 58,
    74, 86, 109, 115, 130, 157
Righteousness, 90, 115, 141, 154,
    162

Sacrifice, 8, 29, 38, 55, 70, 76, 78,
    118, 141, 166
Saints, 53, 89, 121, 158, 160
Salvation, xiii, 8, 13, 16, 53, 60, 62,
    70, 80, 90, 91, 95, 97, 101, 104,
    106, 128, 141, 147, 166

Samaritan, 121–2
Scriptures, ix-x, xii, 33, 93, 130, 144, 150, 151, 154–5, 156
Servant Song, 73
Simeon, 35–6, 64
Sin, 2, 6–7, 11, 16, 19, 23, 28, 32, 38, 39, 56, 59–60, 72, 85, 107, 111, 114, 121, 122, 142, 160
Slavery, 141
Solomon, 23–4
Son of David, 2, 12
Son of God, 55, 95
Son of Man, 72, 74, 92, 117, 130
Spirit, xi, 9, 16, 28–31, 35, 38, 42, 43, 46, 50, 68, 85, 92, 93, 96, 99–100, 101–2, 105, 107, 116, 117, 122, 123, 124, 126, 131, 137, 142, 150, 152, 156, 158, 163, 167
Spiritual, 8, 27, 30, 42, 43, 51, 57, 60, 113, 125, 141, 142, 156, 166
Suffering, 22, 29, 36, 42, 51, 54, 57, 58, 65, 67, 69, 71, 72–3, 77, 78, 80, 85, 86, 90, 91, 126, 132, 148, 150, 158
Synoptic, 74, 164

Temple, 9, 11, 20, 24, 30–1, 35, 37, 38, 39, 55, 56, 60, 70, 75, 82, 122, 152, 156–7, 164
Temptation, 8, 55, 80, 125
Ten Commandments, 141
Thomas, 20, 85
Torah, 17, 20, 94, 154
Transfiguration, 49, 51, 58
Trinity, 101, 121
Truth, 1, 3, 5, 41, 43, 49, 99, 102, 107, 108, 119, 148

Unity, 74, 92, 97, 148, 157

Wisdom, 3, 9, 20, 23–4, 26, 69, 72, 86, 101, 127, 152, 158
Witness, xiii, 74
Worship, ix, 3, 20, 29, 31, 35, 36, 56, 73, 84, 99, 106, 113, 115, 141, 146, 152, 154, 156–7

Biblical references

Old Testament

Genesis, 29, 44, 45, 48, 57, 99, 103, 108, 123, 125, 129, 136–7, 150, 160

Exodus, 6, 23, 29, 38, 49–50, 55, 64, 76, 140

Leviticus, 28, 38

Numbers, 29, 38, 72–3

Deuteronomy, 54, 108, 121, 122, 138

Joshua, 62

Judges, 129

Ruth, 162

1 Samuel, 20, 38, 56, 64–5

2 Samuel, 11, 111

Kings, 24, 55, 105, 108, 111, 113, 116, 117

2 Kings, 11, 49, 116, 119

1 Chronicles, 156

2 Chronicles, 156

Ezra, 32, 34

Nehemiah, 32

Job, 55, 73, 80, 162

Psalms, 1, 11, 16, 19, 20, 56, 97, 113, 138

Proverbs, 59, 101, 136

Ecclesiastes, 127

Isaiah, 5, 13, 14, 16, 18, 28–9, 33, 37, 39, 52, 59, 61, 66, 68, 70, 71, 72, 74, 78, 82, 113, 119, 129, 131, 133, 134, 154, 160

Jeremiah, 1, 11, 22, 43, 108, 131, 133, 134, 136, 138, 140, 142, 144, 146, 148, 150, 166

Lamentations, 73, 88, 146

Ezekiel, 16, 35

Daniel, 95, 158

Hosea, 11, 125, 126, 128

Joel, 52–3, 152

Amos, 52, 121, 122, 123, 142, 144

Micah, 9, 10, 14, 131

Habakkuk, 146–7

Zephaniah, 5, 6

Zechariah, 12, 15

Malachi, 3, 37, 164

Apocrypha

Wisdom of Solomon, 23–4

Baruch, 3

2 Maccabees, 132

New Testament

Matthew, xi, 3, 5, 8, 11, 12, 21, 22, 25, 44, 52, 53, 55, 80, 81, 95, 96, 107

Mark, xii, 3, 33, 55, 58, 60, 83, 95, 107, 116

Luke, xi-xii, 4, 8, 12, 13, 16, 17, 20, 21, 29, 32–4, 37–8, 39, 41, 44, 47, 49, 54–5, 57–8, 60, 62, 64, 68, 70, 82, 83, 89, 95–6, 105–7, 108, 109, 111, 113, 116, 117, 119, 121, 125, 126, 127, 128, 129, 130, 131, 133, 134, 136, 140, 142, 144, 146, 147, 148, 150, 151, 152, 154, 155, 158–9, 160, 162, 164, 166

John, 4, 18–19, 22–4, 30, 31, 32,
46, 49, 64, 66, 67, 70, 72, 74, 75,
78, 79, 80, 82, 83, 84, 85, 86–7,
89, 91–2, 93, 95, 97, 99, 101,
103, 107, 116, 157
Acts of the Apostles, xii, 10, 86, 89,
91, 95, 97, 149
Romans, 20, 27, 45, 54–5, 87,
99–100, 101, 114, 122, 154
Galatians, 26, 105–6, 108, 109,
110, 111, 112, 113, 114–15,
116–18, 119, 120
1 Corinthians, 26, 30–1, 36, 39, 41,
42–3, 44, 45, 59, 68, 72, 76, 82,
103, 105, 119, 157
2 Corinthians, 7, 50, 51, 52, 53, 64,
65, 67, 107
Ephesians, 22, 23, 26–7, 30, 95,
107, 156, 157, 158
Colossians, 20, 26, 64, 121, 122,
123, 124, 127, 128, 166
Philippians, 3, 5, 57, 66, 68, 69,
153
1 Thessalonians, 1, 2
2 Thessalonians, 162, 164
Philemon, 138, 139
Hebrews, 8, 9, 19, 37, 38, 69, 70,
74, 75, 78–9, 104, 129, 130, 131,
132, 133, 136
1 Timothy, 140, 142–3, 144–5
2 Timothy, 146, 148, 150–1, 194–5
Titus, 13, 16–17, 140
James, 109, 116, 124
1 Peter, 80, 82–3
Revelation, 20, 47, 48, 84–5, 86–7,
89, 91, 93, 98